NOT JUST EVIL

MURDER, HOLLYWOOD, AND CALIFORNIA'S FIRST INSANITY PLEA

DAVID WILSON

DIVERSIONBOOKS

Diversion Books
A Division of Diversion Publishing Corp.
443 Park Avenue South, Suite 1008
New York, New York 10016
www.DiversionBooks.com

For more information, email info@diversionbooks.com

First Diversion Books edition December 2016.
Print ISBN: 978-1-68230-327-6
eBook ISBN: 978-1-68230-326-9

AUTHOR'S NOTES

The trial of William Edward Hickman is arguably ground zero in the debate over the potential negative influence of violence and mayhem in movies on the development of young minds. This debate has broadened to include the influence of violent video games, with no clear winner on either side of the argument. What is compelling in the Hickman case is the impact his interest in films had on one of Hollywood's major filmmakers, Louis B. Mayer. The efforts of Louis B. Mayer to protect the image of the film industry are the subject of ongoing debate.

In 1927, when newsreels were a part of the movie-going experience, the murder of Marion Parker by William Edward Hickman shocked a nation. The debate over whether or not the events surrounding his trial should be presented in theaters led to the formation of the Hayes Commission and the first federal efforts to censor the film industry.

Hickman openly admitted that his fascination with

movies influenced his decision to commit murder, and the admission became the basis for his insanity plea. The admission came during the transition from silent films to films with sound. Hollywood was in a state of confusion over how to effectively make the transition. During the trial Hickman's attorneys made no effort to deny he was responsible for the death of Marion Parker. Instead, the defense maintained that Hickman lived in a fantasy world supported by daily visits to the cinema. This addiction to watching movies was the legal basis for his plea of innocence by reason of insanity. This created a second problem for Hollywood, beyond the nuisance of censorship. If the public decided watching a violent movie was harmful to children, the film industry could potentially collapse.

This account of the events surrounding the trial of William Edward Hickman is based on photocopies of trial transcripts, magazines, books, and newspaper articles written between 1926 and 1928. The movie-related material is from the extensive depository of films located at the Margaret Herrick Library of the Academy of Motion Pictures Arts and Sciences in Southern California. This library also provided information on the history of the motion picture industry, and the impact these events had on the efforts by the federal government to regulate the content of films shown in theaters.

This book would not have been possible without the assistance of the employees of the California State Archives, who first found and then provided copies of William Edward Hickman's trial and his appeal. The *Los Angeles Times* was my source for background information on the professional and unprofessional behavior of District Attorney Asa Keyes.

Because this story is nonfiction, all documents are reproduced as they were written, including misspellings and grammatical errors. Some errors indicate the individual's inability to communicate clearly, while others may reflect their state of mind when the quoted correspondence was recorded. The reconstruction of Hickman's life as it pertains to the kidnapping and killing of Marion Parker has been well-documented. Many of the statements made by William Edward Hickman as to his complicity in the kidnapping and murder are contradictory, and appear to be self-serving. As to the question of William Edward Hickman's sanity: draw your own conclusions, just like the twelve citizens who heard all the testimony presented in this book.

CHAPTER 1

"You are talking about the devil incarnate.
Not just evil, but the most evil man I
have ever dealt with in my life. He was an
untalented, mean, vicious, vindictive man."
Helen Hayes, Actress

William Edward Hickman was arrested for the kidnap and murder of Marion Parker in December of 1927. The victim was twelve years old. Her father paid the ransom and found his daughter with her arms and legs removed from her body. The next day gruesome photos of the deceased appeared on the front pages of newspapers across the country. Within a week the crime was the subject of newsreels, shown in movie theaters alongside cartoons and two feature films. The graphic nature of the pictures of the crime scene was unprecedented.

The United States was in the midst of a period of

economic prosperity following World War I. The decade was called the "Roaring Twenties," reflecting an optimistic feeling about the possibilities of positive social change. Prohibition spawned a new style of nightclub called the speakeasy. These clubs featured a new style of music called jazz. Women danced to jazz in a new style of dress called flappers. The country was one continuous party, and no one expected it to stop. The search for the person responsible for the kidnap and murder of Marion Parker shifted the mood of the country.

Before the Great Depression of 1930 devastated America, the state of California was inundated with tens of thousands of migrants hoping to make their fortune in a thriving and diversified economy. Within the geographic boundaries of the Golden State, Los Angeles seemed to offer the most promise, and the city's rapid growth reflected this perception. People moved to Los Angeles looking for a good life, and once they arrived they made every effort to make their dreams come true.

Manhattan Place was one of the alluring communities drawing people to Southern California. It was a residential street lined with single-family homes, well-manicured lawns, and shade trees that the inhabitants cooled under during the hot summer months. When interviewed by local newspapers most residents of Manhattan Place described their neighborhood as quiet and mundane. It was the lifestyle they expected, because they lived in an affluent area they believed was insulated from crime.

On December 19, 1927, just six days before Christmas, all the families living on Manhattan Place lost their innocence. The driver of a black sedan drove down the street looking for the man who was going to pay him a $1,500 ransom. His late-model vehicle stopped alongside a car already parked next to the curb but facing in the opposite direction. The middle-aged man waiting in the car was the father of kidnap victim Marion Parker.

Before a single word was exchanged, the kidnapper pointed a double barrel shotgun out of his car window, the muzzle coming within inches of Mr. Perry Parker's face.

"You see this gun?" The question was muffled by a mask covering the kidnapper's face.

"I see it," the father said, while turning his head in an effort to get a better look at what he hoped was his daughter sitting in the passenger seat.

"Well, did you bring the money?"

As Mr. Parker held up a fist full of twenty-dollar gold certificates in front of the shotgun muzzle, he responded by saying, "Here it is."

The man who was terrorizing the Parker family motioned with his hand. "Give it to me."

"Where's Marion?" the father asked.

"Right here, she's asleep." In the darkness, midway between two streetlights, Mr. Parker could barely make out the face of his daughter seated next to the kidnapper. It was a tricky situation for the distraught father, who had no real choice except to hand over the money. Mr. Parker later stated he thought he saw his daughter look his way, but wasn't sure. He remembered growing impatient with the silence following the exchange. It was as if the kidnapper had stopped to count each bill before deciding what he would do next.

"Are you going to give her to me?" Parker sounded desperate.

"Yes, just as I said. Wait here just a minute."

Regaining his composure, Parker pushed for answers. "How far are you going?"

"Not far."

The kidnapper fulfilled his promise to the father. He drove less than two hundred feet down the street and stopped his car. In the confusion Mr. Parker said he momentarily lost sight of the kidnapper's head and shoulders. He would later testify he heard the passenger-side door slam shut just before the car drove away. Wasting no time, Mr. Parker opened his car door, jumped from his seat, and rushed forward in the hope that his nightmare was over. He was mistaken.

A few hours later at the city morgue, under the illumination of artificial light, Dr. A. F. Wagner pulled back the sheet on the autopsy table to begin his first examination of the night. What he found would disturb him for the rest of his life. It was the body of his next-door neighbor's daughter. Against all odds, in a city of over one million people, Dr. Wagner had been assigned the initial autopsy of Marion Parker before being notified of her death. The doctor was shocked and buckled at the knees. He remembered watching Marion grow up. He had seen her and her twin sister play across the street almost every day for as long as he could remember. After the doctor regained his composure, he spent the rest of the night completing his work because he wanted his report to give the police as much information as possible as soon as possible. The exam was a challenge because most of the body was missing. The examination left

the doctor with feelings of anger and despair. He had never seen such mistreatment of a human body.

The next day he was called back to the morgue and given six additional packages to examine. The contents of each package were held in place by newspaper tied up neatly with black thread. Inside, Dr. Wagner found most of the missing body parts not present during his initial examination of Marion Parker. It took the rest of the day to confirm that each of the body parts belonged to the victim.

After finishing the extensive paperwork needed for a coroner's inquest, the doctor was called to testify before the Los Angeles County Grand Jury. Using a variety of technical terms, Dr. Wagner explained to the members of the grand jury the extent of postmortem mutilation.

> On the first evening I found part of the body, consisting of the head, the trunk down to an inch and a half below the navel, with arms intact but the forearms disarticulated at the elbows. I examined that part of the body. I found that there was also a cut made by a knife on the left on the top of the left shoulder. This cut was two and a half inches long. There were a few superficial marks around this cut, especially between the cuts and the head, which I could not determine at the time as to their cause. They were merely very superficial marks. There were no other marks upon the body at all. There was no discoloration of the face. There were no contusions about the neck. The tongue and eyes were normal, except the eyelids had been raised by a wire running through the hair and brought back and fastened to a ribbon. I examined the organs of the body that were there, the lungs and the heart, the trachea, and I found everything without evidence of contusions or blow. That included also the

stomach, the liver, kidneys, which were all intact, all in perfectly normal, healthy shape.

On the morning of the next day the other parts of the body had been brought in, in separate pieces, each arm, and each leg from the knee down, and also the other part of the body, ranging from an inch and a half below the navel down to the knees. I examined these parts very closely. I could find no evidence of contusion or abrasion or scratches upon the ankles, except very slight, superficial abrasions. The lower part of the body that was brought in contained the genital organs, which were all intact.

Dr. Wagner did not reveal all the details of his examination to the grand jury. Based on instructions from the Los Angeles Police Department and District Attorney Asa Keyes, he left out several important facts from his testimony. The omitted facts would be used to verify any future confessions. High-profile cases frequently motivate false admissions from unstable individuals looking for attention. The omitted information included Dr. Wagner's description of a shirt with the name Gerber written on it and a towel marked Bellevue Arms Apartment. Both items were found packed inside Marion's body cavity.

Within hours of Dr. Wagner's secret testimony, the grisly details were mysteriously released to the press. Many of the nation's newspapers made it the lead story of the day. The preliminary information describing this heinous crime ignited the interest of the public. Newspaper publishers reported that their readers were captivated by every detail of the crime. The public was demanding the identification of a suspect before he attacked another victim.

Propelled by overwhelming public interest, newspapers pulled reporters from other cases and tasked them with digging deeper into the circumstances surrounding the death of Marion Parker. Two days of front-page coverage put pressure on both local and state government officials to apprehend the person responsible for the murder of an innocent child. The lieutenant governor of California, Buron Fitts, received a briefing by the LAPD on the case. He reportedly left the meeting in a somber mood, and wrote a telegram to Governor Clement Young expressing his belief that the case warranted an exception to the state's limit of $2,500 on rewards for information about homicide cases.

The governor, a former teacher, agreed with his lieutenant's assessment. In an act of political theater, he released the lieutenant governor's telegram, hoping to deflect negative public opinion away from himself and onto law enforcement officials. The telegram read as follows:

> Without any doubt the murder of Marion Parker is the most vicious and atrocious crime in California history. California has been stirred as never before, and in view of the nature of the crime most strongly urge, if legally possible that the State immediately offer a thoroughly substantial reward for the apprehension and conviction of the murderer. Suggest that the reward be divided, one-half for information leading to the arrest and conviction and the other half for the actual arrest. Authorities feel that the crime was undoubtedly committed by degenerates and in view of frequency of these crimes recently in Los Angeles on other children and the fact that the criminal is still at large, and the danger from their activities, the State should

be the first one to initiate and contribute its share to the apprehension of these degenerates for the future protection of its children. Unquestionably, the offer of a substantial reward by the State of California and the co-operation with local agents will be one of the most effective weapons in the hands of police authorities.

The *Los Angeles Times* added its support to the governor's call for increasing the reward in Marion's murder case in one of several editorials dealing with the senseless murder:

Staggering to the imagination, abhorrent to every human instinct, are the incredibly horrible circumstances surrounding the murder and mutilation of twelve-year-old Marion Parker, lured from her school-room last Thursday, subjected by her kidnapper to unknown and unnamable horrors, slain, dismembered and—as a crowning, frightful touch to the hell-born scheme of a fiend incarnate—the pitiful fragments of her hacked-up body wrought into the ghastly guise of a living child and delivered to her father in return for $1,500 "ransom."

The police are doing everything possible to apprehend this fiendish slayer, but this is not a job for the police alone. Every citizen of Los Angeles, every resident of the southwest, must assist. If every pair of eyes within the area of the murderer's possible movement is vigilantly alert for a man of his description, for his car and for the numbers of the bills paid him for the little girl's shattered corpse, his chances to elude the gallows will be scant indeed.

The combined support of the LAPD and politicians initiated a nationwide search for an unknown killer. The LAPD literally assigned every officer in the department to the task of identifying a suspect. Chief Davis of the LAPD personally contacted other departments in the state asking for their assistance. Flyers were distributed to customs officials working at the California-Mexico border. The flyers appeared in every bus stop, train station, and post office in the state.

From day one the case was marred with controversy. A local newspaper reported Marion Parker had been taken from her school by a young man without any school official having checked his identity. The public was outraged by the inept conduct. How could anyone abduct a twelve-year-old girl under the direct supervision of school personnel in broad daylight? The kidnapper removed Marion from her school using no physical force or threats. He was unarmed and used only persuasive words and a pleasant demeanor to manipulate those who were responsible for the young girl's safety.

William Edward Hickman walked into Mount Vernon Junior High School shortly after noon and introduced himself to the office secretary using a fictitious name. Naomi Britten got up from her desk, as the man described a terrible automobile accident that had left Mr. Parker, Marion's father, barely hanging onto life at a local hospital. Mrs. Britten would later recall that the young man was well-dressed and polite in every way. There was nothing about him to suggest she was talking to a street-hardened criminal. She overcame her initial shock at the news about the accident and looked for the school's principal, Miss Cora Freeman. Her frantic search failed to find the principal or any other administrator who might help her to resolve the disconcerting situation.

She did locate a teacher in the hallway willing to listen to her predicament.

The teacher, Mary Holt, went to the office to meet face-to-face with the young man who had brought the news of the accident. She described the encounter with the suspect to the principal: "Mr. Cooper (the assumed name of Marion's kidnapper) was very calm and courteous." He told the two women he was employed by the First National Bank, as was Mr. Parker, and he offered to give them the phone number of the bank if they cared to confirm the reason he was there to pick up Marion Parker. His relaxed, almost detached attitude towards the whole situation lasted throughout his visit to the school. When he was introduced to Marion Parker he explained the situation once more, bending at the waist so she could hear him clearly: "Don't cry, little girl, I will take you to your daddy."

On December 20, 1927, just a day after Marion Parker's death, the *Los Angeles Times* printed a statement made by Susan Dorsey, the superintendent of the Los Angeles School District. It read as follows:

> Mrs. Holt had no authority to excuse any child from school. That is done by our vice principal and then only at the request of the child's parents or guardian. But in this case there appeared to be an emergency when the man rushed in and claimed that there had been an accident and the child's father was calling for her.
>
> I talked to Mrs. Holt and am satisfied that I would have acted as she did if I were confronted with the same circumstances. At the time, the vice principal, who is the person in authority entitled to excuse a child from

class, was busy with the Christmas program and could not be reached in the few minutes that elapsed.

The fact that nothing has ever befallen our school children in the past is evidence in itself that they are as safeguarded as is humanly possible.

The statement aggravated an already agitated public. Few parents agreed with Superintendent Dorsey's view of what had happened and what steps were still needed to safeguard the children under her care. Over the next few days, school attendance throughout the state of California fell dramatically.

Despite the confusion, there was one man in the city of Los Angeles who instinctively understood what the death of Marion Parker was going to mean for the city, the state, and the nation. Mr. Asa Keyes, the elected district attorney for the city of Los Angeles, meticulously examined every detail of the kidnapping case. His initial motivation was not justice but opportunity. He felt this was the high-profile case he needed to assure his reelection.

Keyes had spent the previous six weeks of his life putting together a case he hoped would generate political support. The case had its political downside, because it involved some of the most powerful men in Southern California. The crime was the largest fraud in the state's history, described in the press as the C. C. Julian Petroleum Ponzi scheme. The suspects were accused of selling worthless stock to thousands of innocent investors. Some of the suspects unexpectedly praised Mr. Keyes in local newspapers by saying: "I don't believe ten million dollars in his lap would make him violate his oath of office, he has a reputation for honesty that no man would dare question."

On the morning of December 20, 1927, District Attorney Keyes's fate was taking him in a different direction. He cleared his desk of all the documents relating to the stock scandal to make room for the first of several meetings between himself, the chief of the Los Angeles Police Department, James E. Davis, and Herman Cline, chief of detectives. The three men spent several hours discussing the progress on the Marion Parker kidnapping case. Chief Davis and Chief Cline both agreed to assign two of their most experienced investigators, Dick Lucas and Harry Raymond, to Mr. Keyes to assist him in gathering evidence.

Both detectives were physically powerful men, but more important to the district attorney was their willingness to work sixteen-hour days until the case was closed. Mr. Keyes knew their strengths and weaknesses and believed they would do whatever it took to arrest a suspect in the case. Their fixation would not only help Mr. Keyes free the city from fear, it would also bring him one step closer to fulfilling his political ambition of reelection. Keyes located an empty room in his office and ordered that the room be fitted with beds if the detectives needed a place to rest during their investigation.

In contrast, Marion Parker's father was not thinking of the future. Nothing on earth could nullify the suffering and pain associated with losing his child. Two months after the kidnapping he would testify he first came to realize the utter hopelessness associated with the kidnapping on December 15, 1927. It was the day he took a phone call from Naomi Britten, the school's secretary, who was calling to see if the family wanted Marion's twin sister sent home as well. After a few moments of conversation, Mrs. Britten realized she was actually speaking to Marion's father, the man she believed was hospitalized. Mr. Parker quickly responded to her questions with growing concerns of his own. No, he had not been in a car accident, no, he was not injured, and no, he had not sent a man to pick his daughter up from school.

Mr. Parker was under no illusions as he put down the phone and turned to his wife to break the news as gently as possible. His efforts failed miserably. Geraldine Parker fainted after hearing her daughter was missing, possibly kidnapped. For the next couple of weeks Mrs. Parker was watched over by friends and physicians and Mr. Parker was left to deal with the ever-increasing presence of the Los Angeles Police Department in and around his home.

Because the identity of the kidnapper was not immediately known, Detective Lucas and Raymond began their interim report with a timeline of events, starting with the phone call from Marion's school to the Parker's home on 1621 South Wilton Place. They logged into their report a telegram containing one demand: "Do positively nothing till you receive special delivery letter." It was signed: "Marion Parker and George Fox."

The police at the scene asked Mr. Parker a series of increasingly difficult questions about the identity of the man who called himself George Fox. Mr. Parker could only shake his head, telling the detectives that he could not help them. In all of his life, he had never known or met anyone named George Fox. The police found this hard to believe even when it came from a grief-stricken father, so they notified police headquarters to run the name through their database of known criminals and then waited for a reply.

. . .

As the drama surrounding the Marion Parker murder continued to make headlines, an event occurred in Canada that shifted the media attention in a different direction. On Sunday morning, January 9, 1927, in the province of Montreal, Canada, the once-famous Laurier Palace Theater opened its doors to over eight hundred excited children. They came from all over the city to see a special matinee screening of a new silent movie entitled, *Get 'Em Young*. Just moments after the movie projector lit up the darkened theater, the decorative hallways filled with thick black smoke. When the fire alarm was sounded, the response was almost immediate because the fire station was only a few hundred feet from the theater.

It took weeks for fire investigators to determine that the cause of the fire was a discarded cigarette in the basement of the building. In the official report, authorities give credit to the few adults in the audience for their efforts to direct children to the nearest exits. But firemen did find the bodies of seventy-six children who had died from asphyxiation. The reason for the deaths was immediately apparent. Most of the bodies were recovered near an exit door illegally locked from the outside with steel chains.

Canadian newspapers reported that the funeral procession for the young victims of the fire was observed by over fifty thousand citizens who had come to pay their respects. At the church service following the procession, Father Georges Gauthier, the archbishop of Montreal, asked his audience a rhetorical question: "Why was such a place of pleasure allowed to remain open on the Lord's Day?" He also raised the question of the propriety of allowing children to watch motion pictures in the first place. Days after he spoke those words, the Roman Catholic Church of Canada took it upon themselves to start a campaign to prohibit anyone under the age of sixteen from entering a cinema house without being accompanied by an adult. Their reasoning was based on the belief that motion pictures: "ruined the health of children, weakened their lungs, troubled their imagination, excited their nervous system, hindered their studies, and led to immorality in general."

Within a year of the tragedy, following numerous sermons and speeches throughout Canada, the law against children entering theaters without an adult went into effect and remained the law of the land for thirty-three years.

As millions of Americans read reports about the tragedy in Canada, the entire Northeast was recording record-breaking amounts of rainfall from one continuous storm. Farmers from as far off as Tennessee and Missouri were complaining to government agencies that their soil was no longer absorbing rainwater, and by the end of March hundreds of small tributaries of the Mississippi River were overflowing in at least a dozen different states. One newspaper, the *Memphis Commercial-Appeal*, wrote: "All along the Mississippi, considerable fear is felt over the prospect for the greatest flood in history."

On Good Friday, 1927, these fears were realized when the banks of the Mississippi River widened and elevated to previously unrecorded levels. In the process of flowing over the established system of levees, the storm waters "killed 246 people in seven different states while displacing 750,000 people from their homes." The flooding eventually covered and ruined a staggering twenty-seven thousand square miles.

A few weeks later, off the coast of Providence Town, Massachusetts, thirty-seven United States sailors died when their submarine mysteriously sank to the ocean floor. Across the Atlantic, the citizens of Great Britain were trying to deal with an influenza epidemic that had claimed more than one thousand lives in the first week of what would be a yearlong health crisis.

More dispiriting news came from China, where a massive earthquake measuring 8.6 on the Richter scale had killed two hundred thousand citizens and left millions more homeless. In the ensuing weeks, thousands more would die from disease, exposure, and starvation, because rescue efforts by the Chinese government would fail miserably.

During the suffering and despair, Americans still found reasons to celebrate. Charles Lindbergh became a new cultural icon when he flew alone and nonstop from New York to Paris in a plane named the *Spirit of St. Louis*. From Detroit, the Ford Motor Company, one of the country's largest employers, announced the date for the delivery of their mass-produced Model T. The first transatlantic telephone call from New York to London was placed and received with complete clarity. In the Midwest, work on Mount Rushmore started days after the Holland Tunnel opened for traffic connecting the crowded New York City with the ever-expanding state of New Jersey.

On the West Coast, in Southern California, Warner Brothers, Universal, and Paramount announced details of a new process in filmmaking. The process involved integrating pictures with sound. Ground zero for the development of this new technology was a small city on the outskirts of Los Angeles, a scarcely populated community that would soon become known worldwide as Hollywood.

There, among the vast, wide-open spaces, every major motion picture studio built sound stages, working seven days a week and around the clock trying to fulfill the nation's growing desire for films using audible dialogue, sound effects, and music. This overnight transformation made silent films a dead art. Great actors like Charles Chaplin, Gloria Swanson, Mary Pickford, Ethel, John, and Lionel Barrymore, who had captured the collective imagination of the nation, were faced with a tumultuous challenge. Would their voices be accepted by the public, or would they take their places on the cutting room floor alongside the many talented writers, producers, and directors who were unable to adapt?

In the midst of all this change and turmoil, a young man named William Edward Hickman found great comfort and solace sitting in the darkened back row of a movie theater. His need to escape into the fantasy world of film soon became part of his daily routine. He moved from Kansas to Los Angeles in an effort to be closer to the source of his amusement, and was more than willing to commit whatever petty crimes would give him the twenty-five cents a day he needed to indulge his addiction.

For the price of admission he could watch two movies, a cartoon and—the latest additional to the theater experience—a newsreel that included a voiceover description of what was being shown on the screen. Sitting alone in the theater, he would identify with the characters on-screen. He most strongly identified with criminals who appeared to get what they wanted when they wanted it. For him the vision of mean-spirited gangsters meant freedom from domination and control by others. It was a vision that was becoming all-consuming. The trip to the theater became a part of his daily routine, and the three dollars and twenty-five cents he needed each week to feed his addiction became the justification for a life of crime.

• • •

The lead detective on the first day of the investigation of the murder of Marion Parker was Chief Inspector Joseph Taylor. He was a senior investigator in the homicide division and worked directly with the chief of detectives. Because Asa Keyes was immediately involved in the case, Taylor shared responsibility for the investigation with Detectives Lucas and Raymond, who were working directly for the district attorney. It was an awkward allegiance, and both teams knew they were being set up to take the blame if the case was not solved quickly.

The district attorney's detectives had one distinct advantage over Inspector Taylor; they had hindsight. They had heard how Mr. Parker became increasingly agitated during the first forty-eight hours after the kidnapping by what he considered a slow-moving, unproductive investigation. His agitation made Lucas and Raymond suspicious, and the victim's father was included on the first list of suspects.

On instructions from the district attorney, Lucas and Raymond reviewed and documented every move made by Inspector Taylor, and concluded that his team had been remarkably professional from the beginning stages of the inquiry. Before arriving at Parker's home, the inspector had ordered the victim's phone tapped and put all police personnel on full alert. He also notified and instructed all Western Union offices and post offices in Southern California to contact police if anyone tried sending a telegram or special delivery letter to Parker's residence. Police discovered that the kidnapper sent two telegrams and one special delivery letter before the alert went into effect.

Less than forty-five minutes after the first telegram was delivered, a knock on the door of Parker house brought the second of the two telegrams. It read: "Marion secure. Use good judgment. Interference with my plans dangerous." Again the telegram was signed: "Marion Parker and George Fox." Taylor immediately checked the address of the sender and found it to be fictitious.

When District Attorney Keyes read Detectives Lucas and Raymond's initial report, the thing about the situation that disturbed him most was how the grief-stricken Mr. Perry Parker had pleaded with Inspector Taylor to allow him to pay the kidnapper without interference. As in the case of Dr. Wagner, District Attorney Keyes was a friend of Mr. Parker. They knew each other from childhood, and Keyes had known Marion and her twin sister from birth. The district attorney noted that Chief Inspector Taylor suggested to Mr. Parker that the police might actually apprehend those involved in the abduction before it was necessary to furnish the criminals with money. Keys agreed with his detectives that Mr. Parker needed to remain on the list of possible suspects.

Inspector Taylor and Mr. Parker were discussing the issue of ransom at the Parker home when they heard a strong knock at the front door. A United States postman with a special delivery letter sent from the main post office in downtown Los Angeles delivered the note everybody was waiting for:

DEATH

P. M. PARKER

Use good judgment. You are the loser. Do this. Secure 75 $20 gold certificates U. S. Currency 1500 dollars at once. KEEP THEM ON YOUR PERSON. GO ABOUT YOUR DAILY BUSINESS AS USUAL. Leave out police and detectives. Make no public notice. KEEP THIS AFFAIR PRIVATE. Make no search. Fulfilling these terms with the transfer of the currency will secure the return of the girl.

FAILURE TO COMPLY WITH THESE REQUESTS MEANS NO ONE WILL EVER SEE THE GIRL AGAIN. Except the Angels in Heaven. The affair must end one way or the other within 3 days. 72 Hrs.

You will receive further notice. BUT THE TERMS REMAIN THE SAME.

FATE

If you want aid against me ask God, not man.

The kidnapper had made an effort to give credence to his demands by allowing Marion Parker to write a simple statement to her parents in her own handwriting:

Dear Daddy and Mother: I wish I could come home. I think I'll die if I have to be like this much longer. Won't someone tell me why this has to happen to me. Daddy please do what this man tells you or he'll kill me if you don't.

Your loving daughter,
Marion Parker

Mr. Parker was clearly traumatized by the contents of the message. He knew he had broken the kidnapper's first demand by notifying the police as soon as he became aware of his daughter's disappearance. Police could not decide if his emotional reaction to the note removed him from the suspect list or if it was simply a ploy to deflect attention. Parker claimed that all he wanted was to have his daughter returned home safely and that he was prepared to do anything to make that happen. He claimed the amount of ransom money and the apprehension of those responsible did not concern him.

After several hours of heated discussion, Mr. Parker persuaded the LAPD to work behind the scenes while he fulfilled the terms of the ransom note. As instructed he went to work the next day at his usual time and gathered 75 twenty dollar gold certificates. At the end of the day he went home and waited for the kidnapper to give him further details. The first of several phone calls came at 8:00 p.m. Mr. Parker listened carefully to the instructions.

"I am the Fox; have you the money?"

Mr. Parker said yes before the kidnapper cut him off.

"I am some distance away. I will phone you again in a few minutes and give you your instructions."

Thirty minutes later Mr. Parker heard the same voice on the phone. "I am the Fox. Give me your word as a Christian gentleman you will not try to trap me."

There was a pause, but no real response as the kidnapper gave a series of instructions. Mr. Parker was to leave his home and travel several miles until he reached Tenth Street and Gramercy. "And come alone," the voice demanded with authority. "Dim your lights and don't bring any police if you want to see your child alive."

For the first time since Thursday afternoon Mr. Parker felt a degree of hope. On the darkened street, he turned off the engine of his car and waited for the kidnapper to appear. Hours passed without contact. Close to midnight, Mr. Parker gave up any hope of getting his daughter back that night. Completely frustrated and confused about what had just happened, he drove straight home.

The next day, Detectives Lucas and Raymond found the story of Marion's kidnapping on the front page of the *Los Angeles Times* morning edition. By simple process of elimination it was clear someone inside the police department had leaked the details of the case and pictures Mr. Parker had provided to the department as part of the investigation. They knew from past experience that greed could motivate their fellow officers to put the safety of a child aside for financial gain. The two detectives authorized an internal affairs investigation of everyone involved in the case. Mr. Parker remained their only suspect.

At three in the afternoon on December 21, another special delivery letter was brought to the Parker's home. Every attempt by LAPD to catch the person sending the special delivery letters to the house failed. Mr. Parker opened the letter and read the kidnapper's note:

> DEATH Approaching nearer each and every hour P. M. Parker.
>
> When I asked you over the phone to give me your word of honor as a Christian and honest businessman not to try a trap or tip the police you didn't answer. Why? Because those two closed cars carefully followed

your car north on Wilton to 10th and stopped shortly off Wilton on 10th and then proceeded to circle the block on Gramercy, San Marino, Wilton and 10th I knew and you knew what for? One was a late model Buick and the other had disc wheels. Then later, only a few minutes I saw a yellow Buick police car speeding towards your neighborhood. Of course you don't know anything about these facts and that is sarcasm!

Mr. Parker, I'm ashamed of you! I'm vexed and disgusted with you! With the whole damn vicinity throbbing with my terrible crime you try to save the day by your simple police tactics.

Yes, you lied, and schemed to come my way, only far enough to grab me and the girl too. You'll never know how you disappointed your daughter. She was so eager to know that it would only be a short while and then she would be free from my terrible torture and then you mess the whole damn affair.

Your daughter saw you, watched you work, and then drove away severely broken hearted because you couldn't have her in spite of my willingness merely because you, her father, wouldn't deal straight for her life.

You're insane to betray your love for your daughter, to ignore my terms, to tamper with death. You remain reckless, with death fast on its way.

How can the newspaper get all these family and private pictures unless you give them to them? Why all the quotations of your own self, Marion's twin sister, her aunt and school chums? All this continues long after you received my strict warnings.

TODAY IS THE LAST DAY, I mean Saturday, December 17 Year 1927.

I HAVE CUT THE TIME TO TWO DAYS and

only one more time will I phone you. I will be two billion more times as cautious, as clever, and as deadly from now on. You have brought this on yourself and you deserve it and worse. A man who betrays his love for his daughter is a second Judas Iscariot many times more wicked than the worst modern criminal.

If by 8 P.M. today, you have not received my call then hold a quiet funeral service at your cemetery without the body on Sunday, the 18th only God knows where the body of Marion Parker would rest in this event. Not much effort is needed to take her life.

She may pass out before 8 P.M. So I could not afford to call you and ask for your $1500 for a lifeless mass of flesh.

I am base and low but won't stoop to the depth, especially to an ungrateful person.

When I call, if I call, I'll tell you where to go and how to go. So if you go don't have your friends following. Pray to God for forgiveness for your mistake last night. Become honest with yourself and your blood. If you don't come in this good, clean, honest way and be square with me that's all.

FATE FOX

IF YOU WANT AID AGAINST ME

ASK GOD NOT MAN.

Again the kidnapper had decided a short note from Marion Parker in her own hand would verify the authenticity of the letter. That part of the note read:

Dear Daddy & Mother:

Daddy, please don't bring anyone with you today. I'm sorry for what happened last night. We drove wright by the house and I cryed all the time last night. If you don't meet us this morning you'll never see me again.

Love to all,

Marion Parker

P.S. Please Daddy: I want to come home this morning. This is your last chance. Be sure and come by yourself or you won't see me again. Marion.

Detective Lucas and Raymond argued that no further effort should be made to pay the ransom. They knew Mr. Parker was unaware that he had been followed by the LAPD when he tried to pay off the kidnapper. Inspector Taylor made the decision to tell Parker he had been followed on his first attempt to make payment. In a heated conversation, Parker begged the LAPD to give him one last opportunity to meet the kidnapper alone. Eventually Inspector Taylor gave Mr. Parker his word the police would not follow him on his next attempt to deliver the money. Mr. Parker waited for the phone call to set up the exchange. A second special delivery letter was delivered to the Parker home with two separate notes, both sounding irrational.

SIGNED: MARION PARKER DEATH

P. M. Parker

Please recover your senses. I want your money rather than kill your child. But so far you give me no other alternative.

Of course you want your child but you'll never get her by notifying the police and causing all this publicity. I feel however that you started the search before you received my warning, so I am not blaming you for the bad beginning.

Remember the 3 day limit and make up for the lost

time. Dismiss all authorities before it is too late. I'll give
you one more chance. Get that money the way I told
you and be ready to settle.

I'll give you a chance to come across and you or
Marion dies.

Be sensible and use good judgment. You can't deal
with a master mind like a common crook or kidnaper.

Fox Fate

If you want aid against me ask God, not man.

Detective Lucas and Raymond examined and recorded
the second note within the same letter. It read:

P. M. Parker:

Fox is my name. Very sly you know. Set no traps. I'll
watch for them.

All thy and able to handle inside guys, even your
neighbor Isadore B., you know that when you play with
fire there is cause for burns. Now W. J. Burns and his
shadows either remember that.

Get this straight! Remember that life hangs by a
thread and I have a Gillette ready and able to handle
the situation.

Do you want the girl or the 75 $20 gold certificates
U.S. Currency? You can't have both and there's no other
way out. Believe this, and act accordingly. Before the
day's over I'll find out where you stand. I am doing a
solo, so figure on meeting the terms of Mr. Fox or else.

Fate

If you want aid against me ask God, not man.

At the bottom of the second note the kidnapper had
written:

Final Chance.

DEATH

DEATH FINAL CHANCE TERMS

1. Have $1500-75-20 Dollar Gold Certificates-U.S. Currency.

Come alone and have no other one following or knowing the place of meeting.

3. Bring no weapons of any kind.

4. Come in the Essex Coach license Number-594-995 Stay in the car.

If I call, your girl will still be living. When you go to the place of meeting you will have a chance to see her—then without a second's hesitation you must hand over the money. (The slightest pause or misbehavior on your part at this moment will be tragic.)

Seeing your daughter will take a moment. My car will then move slowly away from yours for about a block. You wait and when I stop I will let the girl out. Then come and get her while I drive away—and I won't go slow this time—Dont attempt to follow when you get the girl.

Be sure and wait till my car pulls up ahead and stops and you see me put the girl out before you start up. Don't act excited or think I will run away with Marion.

I will do as I say—

And I hope to God you will have sense enough to do exactly as I have said.

Well, it's not to worry me if you blunder again. I have certainly done my part to warn and advise you.

FATE-FOX

To better understand the kidnapper and his modus operandi, Detectives Lucas and Raymond interviewed several police officers who had been present at the Parker's home when the last special delivery letter arrived. They learned Mr. Parker had received his third phone call from the kidnapper soon after the letters were delivered. Mr. Parker was told by the voice at the other end of the line, in no uncertain terms, that this would be his last chance to save his daughter. Without explanation, the kidnapper hung up the phone, only to call back an hour later. Mr. Parker once again received explicit directions. The new information did not persuade the district attorney detectives one way or another concerning the father's involvement in the crime.

This time Mr. Parker left nothing to chance; he used the rearview mirror in his car from the beginning of his drive to the end to ensure he wasn't followed. Reaching Manhattan Place, he turned his car engine off and waited for the kidnapper to arrive on the deserted street. Thirty minutes later he saw a car pull up alongside him.

Mr. Parker was so traumatized by the events that followed that he could not speak with the police. But Detectives Lucas and Raymond did interview Detective George Contreras, the first officer from the LAPD to arrive at the crime scene. His statement read, in part:

> I walked up to him [Mr. Parker], and asked him where the little girl was and he said, There she is, sitting in the car. Go and look at her. God bless her little heart. And he could talk no more and this friend of his had to take him away. So I immediately went over to the car, and the little girl was sitting up with her little head leaned over to the right, and the first thing that attracted my attention was the thread that was fastened over each eyelid and across the forehead and right back over the

head and down the neck, and sewed onto a white piece of linen that went around the neck. I lowered the little cloth, and there was a cut there, so I did not touch it any more, on account of getting finger marks on it. She had as I say, this linen around her neck and a sweater on, buttoned up, and sat in that position. I made an examination and lifted the body up, and told Inspector Taylor that all of the body wasn't there. He came over and made an examination, and talked to Parker and searched the automobile, and searched the block. And when the coroner came, I carried the body out of the automobile and put it in the wagon, and we came on down to the morgue with it.

The only way for the LAPD to save face amid charges of incompetence was to catch Marion's murderer as soon as possible and bring him to justice. Detective Lucas and Raymond recorded every roadblock set up around Los Angeles. They also noted that the border between California and Mexico was closed and that, with the help of the state police, highways, train, and bus stations were checked around the clock. The problem was they had no suspect and only a vague description.

On the streets of Los Angeles, all available policemen were instructed to stop and question suspicious-looking young men based on information provided by Mr. Parker. The *Los Angeles Times* reported that hundreds of men were questioned, but that less than four dozen were brought in for further interrogation. Among the men who were questioned at length, four suspects were held overnight to verify the facts provided in their interviews.

The normal procedure of holding suspects until their

alibis could be verified was too much for one of the detainees, who suffered from mental disorders. He hung himself hours before being cleared of any wrongdoing. The other possible suspects were all released.

Authorities held a press conference. They admitted to the media that they had no specific suspect. Lucas and Raymond reported Mr. Parker's inability to describe the events on the night of the discovery of his daughter's body to District Attorney Keyes.

CHAPTER 2

"Those wonderful people out there in the dark..."
Gloria Swanson—*Sunset Boulevard* (1950)

On December 17, 1927, twelve months after the formation of the Academy of Motion Pictures Arts and Sciences at the Ambassador Hotel, William Edward Hickman stood in a long line, waiting to buy a ticket to see a feature-length film shown at a theater located a few miles south of Hollywood. Going to the movies was not unusual for the young man. It was a part of his daily routine. What was unusual on that particular day was that several hours earlier he had murdered Marion Parker and then mutilated her body.

As he passed the time, he did his best to appear inconspicuous by making eye contact with everyone who passed the theater. He would explain to the court-appointed psychiatrist that his behavior had been motivated by the fear someone might recognize him as the killer of Marion Parker.

The fact that no one other than himself knew Marion Parker was dead did not diminish his paranoia.

After purchasing his ticket and taking his seat towards the back of the theater, Mr. Hickman momentarily relaxed his guard as his eyes adjusted to the darkness of the room. There was after all nothing unusual about his appearance. At five foot five inches tall and 145 pounds, he was very average, not unlike many of the other young men in the packed theater. His complexion was pale, and his black hair was neatly combed to the side. Normally his hair was very curly, especially in the front, but for his night out on the town he had combed it over and over until it became almost straight in an effort to alter his appearance. He concentrated his attention on the wide screen. It was the reason he had paid twenty-five cents to get into the theater; he wanted the anonymity he felt while watching a motion picture. Months later, while speaking to a court appointed psychiatrist about this particular moment, he said his hope of becoming lost in the moment was not fulfilled. The act of killing Marion Parker was only temporarily erased from his mind.

His statement was recorded for the record and later admitted into evidence in his insanity trial: "The first time I felt sad or had remorse, [for the killing of Marion Parker] was when I was in the Loews State Theater. I broke down and cried while I watched the picture *Forbidden Women*."

The motion picture Mr. Hickman paid to see on the day of the murder was a silent film produced by William C. DeMille, brother of the more famous Cecil B. DeMille. The black-and-white film lasted just over seventy minutes and dealt with issues of betrayal, romance, and a marriage of convenience. Mr. Hickman, who loved all genres of motion pictures and faithfully followed the lives of movie stars, was surprisingly unable to recall the actors or the plot of the film just weeks later during his interview with detectives.

When Mr. Hickman left the theater, he went back to his apartment to complete the final stages of his plan to ransom Marion Parker for $1,500. The fact that she was already dead meant he needed to prepare the body for the exchange. Mr. Hickman believed he could position Marion's body in his car so she appeared to be alive. He also believed Marion's death was Mr. Parker's fault. His actions were justified in his mind by the fact that her father had betrayed him by involving the police in the first attempt to make an exchange.

Hickman made the exchange and returned to his apartment with $1,500 in gold certificates. He was elated; the plan had worked. He cashed in one of the certificates to make sure he had enough money to continue his routine of nightly visits to the cinema. As he went about his daily routine, it became increasingly apparent that he was the subject of a massive manhunt. The original plan had been to stay in Hollywood with enough money to indulge his passion without the nuisance of committing daily petty crimes. But Hickman unexpectedly found himself contemplating leaving the city.

The day after Marion's body was examined in the city morgue, the LAPD sent out an additional 250 policemen to search every street, house, bar, restaurant, park, bus station, and business within ten miles of Manhattan Place. After four exhausting days and nights without any success, Inspector Taylor and his men started retracing their steps. In the late afternoon they surrounded and searched the Bellevue Arms Apartments one more time. They interviewed all the tenants of the building again, including Mr. Hickman, while looking for any possible clues they might have overlooked. During the interview Hickman did not arouse suspicion. This visit from detectives confirmed his lingering belief that he needed to leave town.

As soon as authorities left the building, Mr. Hickman took most of his clothes, all of the ransom money, and three of his four guns and placed them in an inexpensive suitcase. He locked the case in a storage facility near his apartment. After he secured his belongings he walked a couple of blocks and bought a ticket to see a movie at a nearby theater. Inside the theater, he was again unable to relax, but he forced himself to watch the full-length movie. During the film, Mr. Hickman made up his mind to leave the state of California that night.

Within one block of the theater he robbed a man of fifteen dollars, and held the man hostage inside his car for almost half an hour as he drove around town without any clear sense of purpose. Eventually he pulled the car to the curb on Melrose Avenue and released the man before returning to the storage facility to pick up his suitcase. Hickman drove all night, arriving in San Francisco at sunrise.

In Los Angeles, the LAPD reported to the press the apprehension of three new possible suspects in the Marion Parker murder case. There was no daily news item getting more coverage nationwide than the killing of Marion Parker. There were even hourly updates on the radio. All three suspects had confirmed alibis. Detectives reluctantly released the men due to lack of evidence.

The reward money continued to pour into the kidnap fund from every state in the Union, reaching a total of over $75,000. The money failed to generate any leads. Without new information, new evidence, or suspects, the public started drawing their own conclusions. Rumors were rampant, especially in the newspapers, where hundreds of reporters were working on every possible angle of the story. Both the police and the public were becoming increasingly suspicious of Mr. Parker's behavior during the ordeal.

As millions of Americans waited for a break in the case, a single piece of evidence came to the attention of a LAPD detective, who happened to notice a connection between the fingerprints taken from a stolen car and the prints taken from the Bellevue Arms Apartments. Detective Barlow made the following statement hours after his discovery:

"I also took the car prints and compared them with the prints found on the letter. I found them to be identical, even to a small scar discernible only through the microscope."

The detective compared the prints against thousands of fingerprints held by the LAPD. They found that the set matched a known criminal, William Edward Hickman, a man already interviewed in the Marion Parker kidnapping case. LAPD returned to the apartment complex to re-interview the man in apartment 315. They were informed by the building manager that his tenant had unexpectedly abandoned the apartment. Police took additional fingerprints from the room and found several sets matching the prints taken off the stolen car and the prints from the ransom notes.

The police searched Mr. Hickman's apartment and found human hair and tissue in the drain of the bathtub. On the carpet they found a small piece of Brazil nut. It was a significant break in the case. The police had not told the public a Brazil nut shell fragment was found inside Marion's clothes the day they recovered her body. With this new evidence, the LAPD went from working on hundreds of assumptions to focusing on a few hard facts. They packed the entire contents of the apartment and brought it back to the police laboratory for analysis.

Mr. Keyes was elated by the new information and ordered his assistant, Deputy District Attorney Ellis Eagen, to present the grand jury with the case against the suspect. The grand jury heard testimony from Mr. Parker, Naomi Britten, Dr. A. F. Wagner, and Lt. Barlow, the fingerprint expert. They took only minutes to make their decision. Their bill of indictment went directly to Judge Carlos Hardy, who made the following order: "People of the State of California, Plaintiff vs. William Edward Hickman, Defendant, Number 32543. Bench Warrant is ordered issued for the arrest and detention of the defendant. No bail."

With the bench warrant issued, Detectives Lucas and Raymond were optimistic about their chances of gathering enough evidence to secure a conviction. They started by building a comprehensive background check in an effort to find a motive. They soon discovered that William Edward Hickman had been first lured away from his home in Kansas City to Hollywood by his passion for the motion picture industry. Friends and family members all said Hickman had wanted to be near Hollywood, near the actors, and near all things associated with the production of feature-length motion pictures.

Hickman admitted in interviews after his capture that he was a loner who considered the characters on the screen to be his most trusted friends. Mr. Hickman's alternative view of reality proved to be the most rewarding part of his daily existence. The normal behavior of laughing, loving, and even hating, which he felt escaped him during most of the day, came easily to him in the darkness of a theater. He could experience love, rage, and compassion alongside the figures on the screen more easily than he could with real people. His appetite for the movies fed off the chaos he felt in his own life. His daily dose of motion pictures spoke not so much to his need for entertainment as to his need to escape reality and find some semblance of inner peace.

The two detectives believed the need to replace reality with fantasy was not an uncommon desire among many moviegoers. Since the early days of filmmaking, the city of Hollywood had been a place where life was empowered through fantasy, a city where men and women converged daily in the hope of fulfilling their dreams. Even before the first movie had been made in Hollywood, the land itself was the subject of a dream. Horace Henderson Wilcox, a real estate developer, bought over a hundred acres just eight miles from downtown Los Angeles to start a Christian subdivision, where alcoholic beverages would not be sold and where Christian values would be protected by city officials. Even the name Hollywood had significance for Mr. Wilcox, who named the town after a religious friend who had inspired him at an early age.

Mr. Wilcox's dreams never became reality. After a couple of frustrating years, he was forced to sell the land or go bankrupt. After the sale the land was broken into sections. Many of the new owners were filmmakers looking for a sunny location in which to shoot their movies year-round.

Detectives were astonished to discover that Mr. Hickman's love for fantasy and the make-believe world of film never wavered. After kidnapping and murdering Marion Parker he continued his daily trips to the cinema up until the day he left Los Angeles.

Driving through dozens of roadblocks, Hickman decided he was not safe in California. On Sunday December 20, 1927, after traveling continuously for over twelve hours, he arrived in Seattle, Washington, exhausted. He parked his stolen car on the main street and entered a movie theater. At 8:30 p.m., after two hours in the theater, he went to a nearby store and purchased several items of clothing using one of the gold certificates he had received in the ransom. He later told police: "As quick as I looked at that fellow, I knew he recognized me."

The store clerk immediately notified the Seattle police. The Seattle chief of police ordered every off-duty policeman in the department called into work. The manhunt was the largest in the city's history, but it was too late. An hour and a half from the city Mr. Hickman stopped in a small town to steal a new set of license plates for his stolen car.

Early Monday morning, as word of his presence in the Washington and Oregon area was being broadcast around the clock, Mr. Hickman picked up two hitchhikers. He later explained to authorities he had stopped for them in the hope it would throw the police off his trail. He believed if there were two or three men in one car, the authorities would be fooled and not take the time to stop his car. Several hours later, for no apparent reason, he stopped the car and left his two hitchhikers along the side of the road. They walked to the nearest town and saw their driver's picture on the front page of a local newspaper. Badly shaken by the article, they called the police.

The authorities immediately put out an all-points bulletin: "be on the lookout for a stolen Hudson with a California plate number 1-350-391." The notice warned all police agencies that the driver was armed and dangerous.

Mr. Hickman made his trip from California to Seattle and from Seattle to Oregon without once being recognized at any of the numerous roadblocks set up for his capture. An hour after dropping off his first hitchhikers he reached Pendleton, Oregon, where he once again picked up a second pair of hitchhikers, Bill and Jack Merrill.

A local lawman, Chief Tom Gurdane, asked Buck Lieuallen, a state highway patrol officer, to join him in the search for Hickman. The two men sat in Lieuallen's patrol car watching the highway. As Mr. Hickman drove by with his two new hitchhikers, Buck Lieuallen dismissed the car because it had Oregon plates. Chief Tom Gurdane was not willing to ignore the possibility it might be Mr. Hickman. He took a close look at the driver and said: "To hell with the license plate; it's a Hudson and it's green. Get after him."

Two minutes later Mr. Hickman's car was stopped by the side of the road. Neither police officer was willing to take a chance with the three men. They approached the car with pistols drawn. What happened next was reported by the *Los Angeles Times*.

"Was I speeding?" Hickman asked.

Chief Gurdane was not fooled by the man's demeanor. Instead he asked his own set of questions.

"What's your name?"

"My name is Peck."

"Where are you from?"

"Seattle. I've been attending college over there and I'm going to visit my mother."

That was enough small talk for the veteran law enforcement officer to realize he was being conned. "Step out and over to the side." As Mr. Hickman opened the door, his pistol fell and hit the ground. Chief Gurdane looked down, then looked back at his suspect.

"What are you doing with that gun?" he asked.

"It's customary to carry a gun when you are traveling," Mr. Hickman said.

Chief Gurdane shook his head. "Maybe, but you don't need to keep it between your knees."

The two policemen did a quick review of the killer's description and concluded they had their man. Chief Gurdane turned back to the driver and said, "You're Hickman. I knew it was you all the time."

As Chief Gurdane placed Mr. Hickman's hands flat against the hood of the car, he was heard to say, "Well, I guess it's all over."

It was in fact just beginning. Chief Gurdane contacted the LAPD and notified them that he had arrested their suspect. The LAPD notified the district attorney. Asa Keyes scheduled a meeting to discuss the transfer of the prisoner from Oregon to California. The entire criminal justice system in the city of Los Angeles shifted its effort from a manhunt to the collection of evidence for trial.

The young man only realized what was about to happen when he saw the excitement surrounding his capture and confinement. Minutes after the large jail door closed, a curious and unruly crowd of local citizens had formed to get a better look at the most wanted man in America. The *Los*

Angeles Times reported that Mr. Hickman spoke to Lt. Buck Lieuallen saying, "This is going to be interesting before it is all over."

In Los Angeles, members of the news media gathered in front of Mr. Parker's house. They requested a statement from the grieving father. He emerged from his home just long enough to make the following statement: "I am thankful. I am thankful not only for myself but for the parents of all other children that such a dangerous man has been apprehended. This is too terrible a thing to talk about adequate punishment for the man."

• • •

Seven days after William Edward Hickman killed Marion Parker in his apartment, the LAPD stopped investigating the hundreds of crank calls and false confessions and concentrated on one suspect.

On December 21, 1927, the most hated man in America was safely behind bars, and the district attorney of Los Angeles was convinced he would prevail in court. Asa Keyes's confidence was premature. The arresting officer had been the chief of police simply because he was the only officer in the department. He had no training and little experience. He had asked for assistance from the state highway patrol in order to have a partner when he performed the initial search for the suspect. The prisoner was in jail and Chief Gurdane had no idea what to do next.

The lack of training was a problem. William Edward Hickman made a full confession regarding his involvement in the kidnap and murder of Marion Parker. The problem was that the confession was made to a reporter. The suspect was given no opportunity to consult a lawyer, and there was no stenographer taking notes. The confession was based on the reporter's memory of the conversation. Chief Gurdane sent a copy of the confession to the Los Angeles district attorney in the belief he had produced evidence that would lead to a conviction.

Mr. Keyes read a copy of Mr. Hickman's confession within hours after it was given in Pendleton, Oregon. He was horrified. Mr. Hickman claimed he was an accomplice in Marion Parker's kidnapping, and not the actual killer of the young girl. He blamed the murder on a man named Andrew Cramer. He also stated he had made an effort to protect the victim from Cramer. When the district attorney discovered the confession was based on a reporter's interview he flew into a rage. After regaining his composure, he called the LA chief of police and demanded an immediate plan to take custody of the prisoner.

Chief Gurdane was facing the biggest challenge of his career. Outside the jail, hundreds of angry citizens were gathering to confront the man they believed to be responsible for Marion Parker's death. The chief admitted he was in over his head. He worried he was about to lose his prisoner to a lynching party. He knew there was no time to request assistance from the state. Chief Gurdane worked in a small town and knew most of the people who surrounded his jail. He decided to let Mr. Hickman address the mob in the hope they would disperse after their curiosity was appeased.

He was mistaken. The crowd did not leave the street after Hickman was escorted to the front door. Chief Gurdane was desperate. He broke all the rules by promising every person in the crowd the chance to observe Mr. Hickman in jail and safely behind bars, but only if they all agreed to leave and go home afterwards. This questionable tactic actually worked. Hundreds of concerned citizens passed through the jail in single file. As they viewed the prisoner they were allowed to call him names and express their feelings about his alleged behavior. Chief Gurdane apparently had no understanding of the presumption of innocence and no idea how to effectively protect his prisoner.

Back in Los Angeles, Detectives Lucas and Raymond told District Attorney Keyes not to worry about Mr. Hickman's confession. If the suspect was willing to speak with the media, he would be willing to speak with investigators in a proper setting with legal documentation. They both suggested interviewing the suspect on the train ride to California.

Mr. Keyes had a reputation for using his power to bully people into giving him what he wanted. He was by all accounts an impressive-looking civil servant, with a vibrant personality and broad shoulders. He swaggered when he walked across a courtroom. He kept his hair closely cropped, while his cold black eyes were partially hidden by a pair of wire-rim glasses. His reputation was that he acted on impulse. In this case he decided to wait for the official report to be completed before making a statement. Mr. Keyes wanted to close all the holes in his case before the trial started. His reputation as a strict, by-the-book law enforcement officer would be tested over the next couple of months, and he did not want any bad publicity to diminish his chances of reelection.

To accomplish this Mr. Keyes needed to understand

Mr. Hickman's motive for murdering Marion Parker. Legally speaking, he knew the state of California did not require him to present a motive, but he also knew most juries wanted to know why a suspect had committed a particular crime. They wanted to hear a full story.

Detectives Lucas and Raymond were disappointed to discover Mr. Hickman's first confession had not even been elicited by local authorities. Chief Gurdane chose not to take a formal statement from his prisoner after the arrest. Instead he gave a local newspaper reporter named Parker Branin free access to the suspect. Working as a reporter for the *Eastern Oregonian*, Mr. Branin started asking Mr. Hickman a long list of questions as he sat in his jail cell. The suspect told the reporter his part in the kidnapping had been as an unwilling accomplice. Mr. Branin used a notepad and a pencil to paraphrase what he heard.

Mr. Branin's article included the allegation that Andrew Cramer was the true mastermind behind the kidnapping and the man responsible for killing the victim. Hickman claimed he was forced to make his apartment available to Mr. Cramer so Cramer could perform the grisly dissection without detection. In the confession Mr. Hickman tried to paint a picture of himself as the innocent victim of Andrew Cramer's evil intentions.

As quickly as the confession made its way to print, it started to fall apart. Detectives Lucas and Raymond located Andrew Cramer, who provided an iron-clad alibi. For the entire timeline of Marion's kidnapping, Cramer had been sitting in a local jail facing charges of bootlegging.

With no other viable suspect in the case, California law enforcement officials headed north in a private railroad car. Onboard the train were LAPD Chief of Detectives Herman Cline and the two lead detectives, Harry Raymond and Richard Lucas. District Attorney Asa Keyes, the chief of police for Los Angeles, James E. Davis, and a legal stenographer were also added as part of the escort detail. The leadership of the LAPD plus the district attorney were all traveling together to arrest one eighteen-year-old suspect. The effort was unprecedented.

Before the entourage from Los Angeles arrived Mr. Hickman was informed of Mr. Cramer's solid alibi by one of the newspapermen covering his arrest. In response he quickly changed his story, and started suggesting he struggled with mental illness. The *Los Angeles Times* reported Mr. Hickman asked one of his jailers questions about acting insane. Chief Gurdane, who heard about the questions, contacted Dr. W. D. McNary, a local psychiatrist, to interview his prisoner to determine if he was mentally deranged. The chief asked the doctor not to speak with press.

Dr. McNary completed his diagnosis, then broke his promise with Chief Gurdane by speaking with a reporter:

> His mind seemed clear. He told a straight, coherent story and never was at a loss for words. There was nothing about him to indicate insanity. He did not differ a bit from hundreds of thousands of other young men. I found no outward evidence of perversion. Of course, such perversion and inclinations are generally hidden and often difficult to detect. Many persons are afflicted with such inherited traits, but they have the willpower to control their base desires. As to whether Hickman is given to sadistic practices, I cannot tell. I observed him only casually and did not have the opportunity

to make a deep study of him. I saw nothing out of the ordinary about him, nothing that would justify a defense of insanity. He says that he does not like girls, that he is deeply religious, and that his ambition was to become a minister. Several times he made mention of God, and in discussing his capture took the attitude that, since God willed it, it had to be. I would not say that his aversion for women is evidence of perversion. Some men are constituted that way. Nor do I think that his religious convictions are so pronounced as to produce a hallucination that God willed that he commit this act. In our asylum we have hundreds of patients who are suffering from delusion that they are in communication with Jehovah.

As if this were not prejudicial enough, the doctor continued to express his opinion in general about Mr. Hickman's state of mind:

It is a most difficult matter for society to protect itself from degenerates. Their perversions are generally hidden. They crop up occasionally in some of the appalling crimes, which fill the front pages of our newspapers. To discover, to weed out, to emasculate these people, both as a remedy and protection for society, would be a most difficult matter. Young Hickman might have come to Pendleton, established himself here, gained a good reputation, and if he were afflicted with sadist desires, might have controlled them for an indefinite period. To discover these fellows before they commit their awful crimes is almost impossible.

Chief Gurdane appeared incapable of following well-established police protocol. He further confused the legal situation by allowing the Reverend W. H. Robins to interview his prisoner. While it is acceptable for a prison to ask for religious guidance, it is not all right for the content of such a meeting to be released to the media. The man of the cloth spoke with the suspect and gave several newspapers and a newsreel camera crew a blow-by-blow account of his conversation:

> He asked me if I thought God would give him a chance. I told him the government of the country can punish crimes but not sin, because sin is against God. At that point, he broke down and cried for some time, and I feel convinced that his actions were not hypocritical. I then gave a prayer of two or three minutes. He acted as a perfect gentleman all the time I was with him. I would not definitely say that he is religious, although it is quite evident that he has religious training. He speaks excellent English and is well educated in some respects, although I would say his education is somewhat lopsided.

The minister was asked by one of the newsmen to elaborate upon his comments. His response made reference to the very first case of murder in the United States in which the defendants successfully used the insanity plea to escape a death sentence:

> You must understand, I am not giving my opinion as to whether or not he is guilty of murder. But I think it's the same rotten philosophy fed to Leopold and Loeb that is responsible for the situation. I believe also that if any blame is to be placed, we may say that those who gave these behavioristic teachings to this young man are responsible.

The comment about Leopold and Loeb was a reference to Nathan Freudenthal Leopold and Richard Albert Loeb.

In 1924 both young men had been attending college at the University of Chicago. They kidnapped and murdered a fourteen-year-old boy named Robert Franks. Their admitted motive was to prove they had the intellectual sophistication to commit the perfect crime. The closing argument by their well-known attorney Clarence Darrow resulted in a sentence of life in prison rather than the death penalty. The efforts of Clarence Darrow ignited a public debate over the morality of the death penalty, with the majority of Americans at the time of the trial believing the two suspects had avoided execution because of their social status and not because they deserved leniency.

Chief Gurdane made a final lapse in good judgment by allowing Mr. Hickman to make a written statement before taking the opportunity to consult with a lawyer. The statement read as follows:

> This affair has gained nation-wide publicity and the great reward and search by the police of the west coast, shows the opposition of American people to criminal tendencies. Kidnapping and savage murders are the worst of American's crimes and everything should be done to prevent anyone interfering in any way with the liberty and life of American citizens.
>
> Young men and college students should consider the Parker case as a typical crime of the worst that can happen when a young man gradually loses interest in family, friends and his own honesty.
>
> The young men of this country can see that I can pass as an ordinary young man as far as outward appearances go.
>
> Crime in its simplest definition is to have without

work and enjoy the same place in society as other people and still show no honest effort or intention to go right.

Young men, when crime has once overcome your willpower to be honest and straight you are a menace to society. Take my example to illustrate this. See how I tried to get what every young man wants, but in becoming a criminal to do so I put my own life in a mess and the way out is dark.

I hope I can do some good by giving you this warning. Think it over, see my mistake. Be honest and upright. Respect the law. If you do these things you'll be happier in the end and you will have gained much more from your life.

While the escort team made its way towards Pendleton, Oregon, Chief of Police Davis and Chief of Detectives Cline made statements to the press in an effort to counter the remarks made by Hickman. "There is little doubt," Chief Davis said to newspaper reporters, "that there will be great change in Hickman's story; now he will have to prove his assertions to me and my men, who are familiar with the brutality of the Parker murder and kidnapping."

When Cline was asked his opinion he responded in kind. "The story of Hickman involving an accomplice is an absurdity. We have checked every angle of his asserted accomplice and have found the story false and weak. We are after the truth of the matter, and I am convinced we shall find it when Hickman is faced with the facts by those who know the intricate details of the Parker crime. Hickman already has his neck in the noose."

As the time approached for transferring the prisoner, Chief Gurdane put him on suicide watch. Already suffering severe criticism for his handling of the case, Chief Gurdane did not want William Edward Hickman to die in his custody. The record shows that over the next twelve hours Gurdane's prisoner made at least two ineffective attempts to kill himself. The first came when he jumped off the top bunk in his cell, falling headfirst onto the cement floor. The fall resulted in a nasty headache. The second attempt involved hanging himself with a small handkerchief. The noose broke, and Hickman suffered no injury.

On Christmas Day, just moments before the Los Angeles escort entered the hallway of the Oregon jail, Mr. Hickman was reported to have said: "I've got the worst of it ahead of me. They are trying to hang me before they get me. They won't give me a chance to tell my story and get cleared. I'm away up here and I haven't got a friend. They're right down there, where they can have everything fixed up by the time I get back."

What no one was reporting was the possible connection between Mr. Hickman and Mr. Perry Parker. When Detectives Lucas and Raymond built their timeline of Hickman's life they discovered records showing Mr. Hickman's criminal career had began at the age of seventeen, when he and a friend robbed a candy store in Kansas. They used the money from the crime to finance a trip to the West Coast. Before reaching Hollywood they found the cost of traveling across several states to be more expensive than they had originally thought. They took this problem in stride, and started robbing stores as their financial needs dictated. They committed over a dozen robberies before reaching Los Angeles. During their first robbery attempt inside California's borders, they unexpectedly ran into a police officer named D. J. Oliver, who was visiting the pharmacy they wanted to rob. A gunfight quickly ensued. Mr. Hickman and his friend left the drug store pharmacist dead and the policeman seriously wounded.

The pharmacy was their first unsuccessful robbery, and it literally scared both men into applying for honest work a few days later. The First National Trust and Savings Bank offered both men jobs just after New Year's Day, 1927. Mr. Perry Parker was a senior officer with the bank. Mr. Hickman and his friend were given such inconsequential jobs that Mr. Parker did not remember him until a bank customer's checking account ended up four hundred dollars short. The paper trail led directly to Mr. Hickman, who was arrested, tried, and convicted of fraud based on evidence obtained from Hickman's own confession. In Los Angeles juvenile court, Judge Carlos Hardy sentenced Hickman to probation and restitution. Mr. Hickman immediately applied to get his old job back at the bank, but was turned down.

In interviews with detectives, Mr. Parker stated he did not believe Mr. Hickman's discharge from his position with the bank was the motive behind the kidnapping.

> I recall the unusual manner in which Hickman talked with me about his discharge for forgery. I remember how he asked me for his position again after being granted probation, which probation I protested, and his replies to questions, with calm manner and voice I heard over the telephone, and lastly the coolness and nerve displayed Saturday night when we met for the exchange and I am convinced that Hickman was at the other end of the telephone and that he took the $1,500. I cannot call to mind any words of madness or revenge

that passed while I was talking with Hickman, but I do remember that his reaction to the forgery charges did not seem to me to be usual. He evinced no nervousness and showed very little concern over the seriousness of his actions. This impressed me very much at the time, but no thought of his planning to harm me or members of my family in return for his discharge entered my mind.

After Hickman's trial on forgery was concluded, the young man had enough money for a train ticket back to Kansas City. With court approval, he left California, returned home, and took a part-time job in a local movie theater as an usher for the evening shows. While a movie theater was an ideal place for Mr. Hickman to enjoy his favorite pastime, he did not like keeping to a work schedule. People who knew him said he suffered from depression and a strong feeling of hopelessness and inadequacy. After he was fired from his job as an usher he bought a gun, breaking the first of many legal restrictions placed on him by the probation department in Los Angeles.

Over the next two months Mr. Hickman used his new gun to commit forty-three armed robberies in five different states. This string of high-risk criminal actions was for one purpose: to earn the money he needed to get away from Kansas. Mr. Hickman let a few family members know he wanted desperately to get back to Southern California, but they had no idea how he earned the money to make the move.

Mr. Hickman returned to Hollywood in the middle of November 1927, where he quickly picked up his old habit of robbing as a means of making a day-to-day living. He decided he needed to make one big score, something more than what he was making from each robbery. William Edward Hickman saw kidnapping for ransom as the means to this end. He remembered how there had always been money available to the staff at the bank. He first focused on Mr. Harry Hovis, a senior executive with the bank who had a young child. But Hickman decided the child was too young and would be difficult to keep quiet. Then he remembered Mr. Perry Parker and his twin daughters, Marion and Marjorie. One of them would be the perfect victim.

CHAPTER 3

"In the beginning was the Word."
John 1:1

The legal team heading towards Oregon was sensitive to media coverage, because they all understood that the mood of the city was not tolerant of incompetence in law enforcement. Los Angeles had spawned a number of reform movements in reaction to the intimate relationship between bootleggers, politicians, and law enforcement. Three years earlier, in 1924, Congress had passed the Volstead Act, making the sale of alcohol illegal in the United States. It soon became apparent to the public that the law was a bad idea, but legislators were slow in moving towards repeal because of the huge amounts of money being made through graft and corruption. At the time of Hickman's arrest Prohibition was still the law of the land, and any pretense at effective law enforcement was the exception rather than the rule.

The debate on repeal was long past the point that the public simply opposed the idea of making alcoholic beverages legal. The issue was now eliminating the systemic corruption following in the wake of the ill-advised ban on drinking. District Attorney Keyes was aware of the public sentiment. During his first year term he had fired sixty of the eighty-seven employees working in his office. He also successfully prosecuted a number of Los Angeles councilmen for accepting bribes. His efforts to arrest members of the Klu Klux Klan involved in bootlegging led to the passage of legislation banning the organization from the state of California. Keyes's persona as champion of law and order was popular among the citizens of Los Angeles, but also created serious opposition from politically influential businessmen with ties to organized crime. The ambitious district attorney did not want to give his enemies reason to challenge his bid for reelection. The process of bringing William Edward Hickman to trial needed to be a textbook case of proper procedure and correct legal protocol.

Keyes was especially sensitive to the fact that he was dealing with a kidnap case. Two years earlier the popular evangelist Aimee Semple McPherson had claimed to have been kidnapped and taken to Mexico, where she was held awaiting the payment of a ransom. McPherson claimed she escaped from her captors, walked across the Senora desert, and made her way to Arizona. Keyes believed the story about the kidnapping was a lie, told to cover an illicit affair with a member of her staff. He charged her with perjury, and in the midst of a huge media circus, the charges were dropped. The scandal was one of the reasons Keyes wanted a clean case, with a clear villain and a clear road to resolution and justice.

Each of the individuals chosen by the district attorney to escort William Edward Hickman from his jail cell in Pendleton back to Los Angeles was well aware of their boss's concerns. The next phase of their investigation would depend largely on their suspect's willingness to cooperate. The entire team wondered what the accused killer would be like when they met him for the first time. Most assumed he would be heartless and cruel. What they did not know was whether Mr. Hickman would be accommodating or temperamental.

Several reporters recorded that first meeting in great detail. Chief of Detectives Cline stated he found Mr. Hickman disappointingly simple and later recalled their first meeting in sworn testimony:

> We called him out. The door was being unlocked, and we wanted to talk to him. He did not make any response at first, and if I remember right, one of the officers or someone attached to the jail went in and took him by the shoulder and kind of shook him and told him to come out, the Los Angeles officers were there. And he came out and immediately went into hysterics.

Chief Cline also reported that Hickman's small, pale body commenced to jerk as he cried out, in a loud tone of voice, "calling over and over again to Marion, Marion, Marion. Then Mr. Hickman looked around the room before violently trying to get at somebody, or get away from something."

Reporters from both the *Los Angeles Times* and the *New*

York Times saw things differently. They described one Los Angeles detective treating Mr. Hickman with verbal disdain and chiding him more than once to behave like a man. Regardless of the differences in these recollections, one of Asa Keyes's earlier statements was taken down word for word and never disputed: "Of course he's not insane. He is merely assuming that pose, I assume, for mercy. Tonight Mr. Hickman will tell me the truth of the Parker killing." Mr. Keyes was only half right. William Edward Hickman did not confess that first night because the escort team's departure was postponed for a day, until the day after Christmas.

The effort by the escort team to get Mr. Hickman to make a binding confession started at the jail in Pendleton, Oregon, on December 26, when Detective Raymond spoke in a blunt and bombastic manner. "Get his things and let's get out of here." He made the statement as if addressing his partner, Detective Lucas. Before Detective Lucas could respond, Detective Raymond turned towards Mr. Hickman and ordered him to act like a man and to get up off the floor where he was crying. Detective Lucas immediately took up the role of "good cop" in the scenario. "Slow up Harry. This boy's got his problems. Let the fellows clean him up a little; he has his pride you know. There are a hundred cameramen waiting for him outside. Don't take him out looking like a bum." Mr. Hickman's apparent need for sympathy and attention was soothed by those flattering words.

The good-cop-bad-cop ploy worked on Hickman as Detective Lucas pretended sympathy for the young man's hopeless situation. Raymond immediately backed off so Lucas could take the role of lead detective in the interrogation. But before they could start they needed to get their prisoner past the reporters, newsreel cameras, and the unruly crowd outside the jail. As a safety precaution Raymond and Lucas handcuffed themselves to Hickman's wrists. The motorcade with Hickman and his escort team made its way from the jail to the train station without incident.

Once they were all onboard the train, the questioning of Mr. Hickman started in earnest as Raymond picked up where he had left off, pushing the impressionable young man. "Did you hear that mob?" he asked, not waiting for an answer. "As far as I'm concerned, I would just as soon let them have you."

Then Lucas knew it was his turn. "Oh, shut up. Quit punching. How do you know, he might beat the case; you're not the jury."

Lucas turned and started asking Mr. Hickman a series of pertinent questions. The short young man was still sandwiched in between the two bulky detectives. His defense lawyers would later claim their client never stood a chance. Within two hours of leaving Pendleton, after being repeatedly asked the same questions over and over again, the two determined detectives and the ambitious district attorney received what they wanted: a full confession from William Edward Hickman about his role in the kidnapping and murder of Marion Parker.

The other members of the team were quickly called into the Pullman compartment to hear Mr. Hickman's verbal confession. His vivid and detailed remarks gave the district attorney all the important dates, times, and places relating to the actual crime. Detective Lucas reported that Mr. Hickman behaved amiably towards everyone during the entire process and watched them all sign the document as witnesses to the actual confession.

After a brief conference between the DA and the detectives, several sheets of paper and a pencil were placed in front of Mr. Hickman, who was asked to complete a second statement explaining in his own words the motive behind his criminal behavior. The significance of this move was not lost on anyone who was watching. Asa Keyes could barely hide his excitement as Mr. Hickman picked up the pencil and started writing. The district attorney had physical evidence linking his suspect to the body of Marion Parker, along with a complete confession and the handwritten statement describing his motives. Mr. Keyes could now see how the court case would unfold, and there was no way it was going to result in anything less than a death sentence.

The transcript of Mr. Hickman's formal confession read as follows:

> My name is William Edward Hickman. I was born February 1, 1908, at West Hartford, Arkansas. I desire to make the following statement relative to the kidnapping of Marion Parker in Los Angeles, Thursday, Dec. 15, 1927.
>
> During the past six months the idea of kidnapping a young person and holding it for ransom came to me as a means of securing money for college. I had already been in touch with President Hawley of Park College, near Kansas City, Mo., and was to see him again in the February following to arrange my entrance.
>
> On November 23, 1927, I rented an apartment at the Bellevue Arms house under an assumed name of Donald Evans. At this date I had no definite plans to

kidnap, but on Monday, December 12, I decided to locate Mr. Harry Hovis, chief teller at the First National Bank of L.A., and arrange to take his young child, but I wasn't satisfied with the situation. I then thought of Mr. P. M. Parker, because I had seen a young girl with him one day at the bank while I was employed there as a page. This was the First National Bank at 7th & Spring Sts., and since I thought that the girl with Mr. Parker was his own child, I decided to start my plans.

On Wednesday, Dec. 14, I drove out to Mr. Parker's house at 1631 South Wilton Pl. and waited to see him drive home and his daughter return from school.

On Thursday, Dec. 15, 7:30 a.m. I was again parked near the Parker residence in my car, which I had stolen in Kansas City, Mo., early in November. It had a California license plate, No. 1,677,679, which I took from a Chevrolet car in San Diego, Sunday night, about the 5th of December. About eight o'clock I saw two young girls leave the Parker home and follow them to the Mt. Vernon Jr. High School in that district. I returned to this school later from my apartment at the Bellevue Arms. I entered the attendance office at approximately 12:30 and asked for Mr. Parker's daughter, saying that her father had been in an accident and wished to see her. I gave my name as Cooper and assured the teacher that I was a friend of Mr. Parker's and worked at the First National Bank. I was asked if the girl's name was Marion Parker since it occurred that Mr. Parker had two daughters at the school. I replied in the affirmative and emphasized that it was the younger daughter for whom the father was calling. There was only a slight wait and when Marion was called from her class. I told her to come with me, repeating what I had said to the teacher.

The young girl did not hesitate to come with me and we left the school immediately. I drove east on Venice Blvd. to Western Ave., north on Western to Beverly Blvd., east on Beverly Blvd., to Temple St., on Temple to Glendale Blvd., out Glendale Blvd. through the city of Glendale.

I stopped the car on a quiet street out in this vicinity and told Marion that she had been deceived. I told her that I would have to hold her for a day or two and that her father would have to give me $1,500. Marion did not cry out or even attempt to fight. She pleaded with me not to blindfold or tie her, and promised not to move or say anything. I believed her and took off the blindfold and the bandages from her arms and ankles. I explained to Marion what a chance I was taking. I warned her that she would be hurt if she tried to get away, and I showed her my .380 automatic. Marion said she understood and that she didn't want to be shot. I started the car and we drove back to Los Angeles, to the main post office, where I mailed a special delivery letter to Marion's father. Marion sat right up in the seat beside me and talked in a friendly manner. It was very nice to hear her and I could see that she believed and trusted me for her safety. When I left the post office, I drove out to Pasadena. Here I stopped at the Western Union office on Raynold Avenue and left Marion perfectly free in the car while I sent a telegram to her father. I wanted to warn Mr. Parker not to do anything until he got my letter, and told him that his daughter was safe.

Marion and I left Pasadena and drove out Foothill Blvd. beyond Azusa. We talked and had a jolly time. Marion said she liked to go driving and she went so far as to relate to me that she had a dream just a few days before that someone called for her at the school and in reality kidnapped her. Before dark came I turned back and we stopped in Alhambra where I mailed a second telegram. At seven o'clock we went to the Rialto Theater in South Pasadena, and saw the picture entitled *Fathers Don't Lie*, with Esther Ralston. Marion enjoyed the picture and we both laughed very much during the vaudeville, which followed the picture.

We left the theater about ten p.m. and drove directly to the Bellevue Arms Apts. Marion, I could see, was a little worried and also sleepy. We sat in the car by the side of the apartments for about thirty minutes and saw a chance to enter without being seen. I told Marion that my room was on the third floor and cautioned her to follow just a few steps behind me. No one saw us go to my apt. (No. 315) and when we were inside Marion went to sleep immediately. She chose to sleep on the couch and only took off her shoes, and used a pillow and a heavy blanket, which I gave her for cover. I placed a reading lamp by the door and left it lighted so that it cast a dim light over the room. I slept in the bed and retired shortly after Marion. I stayed awake for some time, to see that the girl would not attempt to leave the apt.

Next morning Marion was awake by seven o'clock. She was sobbing and didn't say much. I got up and prepared breakfast, but she wasn't hungry.

After a while I began to talk to Marion and tried to console her. I told her that she could write a letter to her father and that I would also. So then she stopped sobbing and wrote the note and didn't cry any more that day. About 9:30 a.m. I left the apt. for about thirty minutes. I went downtown, where I got the newspaper and mailed the second special delivery letter, which included Marion's note. I tied Marion to a chair while I was gone but used cloth bandages and she was not cut or bruised in any way. I did not blindfold or gag her and she promised to keep quiet.

When Marion saw her pictures and name in all the papers she felt sorry, because she didn't want her father to give out the news of her kidnapping because I had told her all of my plans. Later however she seemed to like to look at her pictures and kept reading the account of her abduction. Marion didn't want to stay in the apt. all day so I promised to go out driving again. We left the apt. about noon and drove out through Alhambra and San Gabriel, past the Mission Playhouse to San Gabriel Blvd. and turned on the highway towards San Diego near Whittier. We drove through Santa Ana and while we were stopped there for gasoline at a Richfield station I noticed that the attendant looked at Marion very closely. We drove on beyond San Juan Capistrano and stopped to rest the car a while before we turned back. We were about 70 miles out of Los Angeles and it became dark before we got back to the city.

I secured some evening papers and Marion read to me as I drove. About 7 o'clock I stopped the car just south of 7th Street on Los Angeles St. and left Marion in the car while I went to the P. E. Station at 6th and Main St. and called her father over the telephone. I called twice but the line was busy each time. I told Marion so we then drove up Los Angeles St. to Sunset Blvd. and out Sunset to a drug store near Angeles Temple. I called Marion's father and talked to him. He said he had the money and wanted me to bring his girl back to him. He said he'd meet me anywhere and I said I'd call back. I called the second time from a drugstore at Pico and Wilton Sts., at about 8:30, which was about 30 minutes later than the first. I told Mr. Parker to get in his car alone and drive north on Wilton to 10th and turn to the right one short block to Gramercy, just north of 10th. Marion and I were parked on Pico, between Wilton and Gramercy and we both saw Mr. Parker drive by. There were two other cars following his, and I feared that some detectives were planning to trap me, so Marion and I drove directly back to my apt. and didn't go by her father. We got back inside without anyone seeing us. Marion sobbed a little because she couldn't go home that night but she saw everything and was content to wait till the next morning. Marion slept the same way Friday night as Thrusday and we both were awake and up by 7:30 the next morning.

I told Marion to write her father that he must not try to trap me, or something might happen to her. She wrote the note in her own words and very willingly, same as the first note, since she knew my plans as well as I did and read all of my letters. I told Marion all along that I would have to make things look worse to her father than they really were, so that he would be eager to settle right away. Marion knew that I wrote her father that I would kill her if he didn't pay me, but she knew that I didn't mean it and was not worried or excited about it. In fact, I promised Marion that even though her father didn't pay the money, I would let her go back unharmed. She felt perfectly safe and the tragedy was so sudden and unexpected that I'm sure she never actually suffered during the whole affair, except for a little sobbing, which she couldn't keep back for her father and mother.

I wrote my third letter to Mr. Parker and put it with Marion's note in the same envelope. I told Marion that I would go downtown again and get the newspapers and mail the special delivery letter. I said I would return in less than a half hour and then we would get in the car and meet her father somewhere that morning.

I went ahead and tied her to the chair as I did Friday morning, except that I blindfolded her this time, and made ready to leave the apt. She said hurry and come back.

At this moment my intention to murder completely gripped me. I went to the kitchen and got out the rolling pin, meaning to knock her unconscious. I hesitated for a moment, and changed my mind. Instead I took a dishtowel and came back to where she was sitting on the chair, pushed back in a small nook in the dressing room, with her back turned to me. I gently placed the towel about her neck and explained that it might rest her head, but before she had time to doubt or even say anything I suddenly pulled the towel about her throat and applied all of my strength to the move. She made no audible noise, except for the struggle and heaving of her body during the period of strangulation, which continued for about two minutes.

When Marion had passed to unconsciousness and her body stopped its violent struggle, I untied the bandages and laid her on the floor. I took off her shoes and stocking, her sweater and dress, and placed her in the bathtub. I got a big pocketknife, which I had in the apt. and started cutting. First, I cut a place in her throat to drain blood, but this was not sufficient. I then cut her arms in two at the elbows and washed and wrapped them in newspaper. I drained the blood from the tub as I cut each part, so that no stains would be allowed to harden. Next, I cut her legs in two at the knees. I let the blood drain and then washed and wrapped them in newspaper also. I put the limbs in the cabinet, in the kitchen, and then took the remaining undergarments from the body and cut through the body at the waist. As I cut the limbs and body there were heavy issues of blood and jerks of the flesh to indicate that life had not completely left the body.

I drained the blood from the midsection and washed and wrapped this part in newspaper and placed it on the shelf in the dressing room. I washed the blood from the tub and separated some of the internal organs from the body and wrapped them in paper. Then I tied a towel about the neck and tied another towel to it and left the upper part of the body to hang until the blood had completely drained from it. I placed a towel up in the body to absorb ant blood or anything, which did not dried. I took this part of the body and, after I had washed and dried it, wrapped the exposed ends of the arms and waist with paper and tied them so that the paper would not slip. I dressed the body and placed it in a brown suitcase. I combed back the hair, powered the face, and laid a cloth over the face when I closed the suitcase. I put the suitcase on a self in the dressing room and then cleaned up the bath, trying not to leave any traces of blood anywhere.

I went to the writing desk and wrote a second part to my third letter, which I called the final chance terms. I opened the envelope, which I had sealed, and put this third part with Marion's second note and my third letter. I then went downtown and mailed this letter special delivery to Mr. Parker about one o'clock. I then went to

Loew's State Theater, but I was unable to keep my mind on the picture and wept during the performance.

I returned to my apartment about 5:30 p.m. and took all the parts of Marion's body downstairs to the car waiting by the side entrance. No one saw me and I hurried out Sunset Blvd. and turned to the right at Elysian Park where within 100 yards along the road I left all of these parts.

I was back in the apt. by 6 o'clock and took the suitcase with the upper section and drove to Sixth St. and Western Av. Here I called Mr. Parker and told him to come to Manhattan Place and park just north of 5th St. I drove around in that neighborhood to see that no police cars were coming before I met Mr. Parker and I stopped between Sixth and Fifth Sts. on Manhattan Place and took the body from the suitcase. I left the suitcase outside the car and before I got back inside I turned one number back from each end of the rear license plate. About eight o'clock I saw Mr. Parker's car where I had told him to be and as I approached I tied a white handkerchief about my face. I drove up to the side of his car and stopped. I had a shotgun in one hand and I raised it up so that Mr. Parker would see it and cautioned him to be careful. He asked to see his daughter and I raised up the head of the child so that he could see its face. He asked if it was alive. I said, "Yes, she is sleeping." I asked for the money and he handed it right over to me. I said I'd pull up ahead of him about 50 feet and let the child out. I pulled up ahead and stopped but only leaned over and placed the body on the edge of the fender so that it rolled over onto the parked and then I speeded east on 4th Street and downtown where I parked the car at 9th and Grand.

Note: The knife that I used in the cutting of the child was purchased at a hardware store on South Main Street about 5th Street. I identified this knife to Chief of Detectives Cline, who now has it in his possession. He got this knife from my suitcase where I said it was.

I then went to the Leighton Café in the arcade on Broadway, between 5th and 6th Sts. I passed one of my twenty dollar gold certificates when I paid for my meal.

I went back to the apt. after I left the cafeteria and retired. On Sunday morning detectives from the police dept. searched my apt. for towels but made no arrest. I took my guns and the ransom money and checked them at the P. E. Station near 6th and Main. I also checked a black handbag and a suit box at the station. I went to the Tower Theatre early in the afternoon. Shortly after five p.m. I rode out on Hollywood Blvd. on a P. E. car and got off at Western Ave. I entered a closed car parked on Hollywood Blvd. near Western and told the man sitting at the wheel to start the car. He saw my gun and obeyed. We drove several blocks away and I told him to leave the car. Before he did so I took about $15 from him in money. This occurred about six o'clock Sunday evening, and shortly after seven I had secured my packages and grip from the P. E. station and was on my way out of Los Angeles on Ventura Blvd. I drove overnight and arrived at San Francisco Monday about one p.m. I stopped at the Herald Hotel and Tuesday about 9:30 a.m. I started for Seattle, Washington. I arrived there between 6 and 7 p.m. Wednesday and left about 9:30 p.m. to go back to Portland. I passed two of the gold certificates in Seattle and another on the road about twenty miles south of Seattle. The two bills in Seattle were in the downtown district, one at a clothing store where I purchased a pair of gloves and a suit of underwear, the other was at a theater.

Note: While at the Herald Hotel in San Francisco, room 402, I assumed the name of Edward J. King, of Seattle. I arrived in Portland early Thursday morning and started on the Columbia River Highway east. Before leaving Portland I left my California license plates and put on two Washington plates, which I took from a Ford car in Olympia. On the Columbia River Highway near he Dalles I picked up two boy pedestrians and drove on till within a few miles of the town of Pendleton, Oregon, where I was arrested and taken to the city jail at Pendleton. The statement that I made after arrest implicating Andrew Cramer and June Dunning was false. This is my true statement.

Note: On the highway north of San Francisco I picked up a man and left him at Redding, I picked up two fellows south of Dunsmuir who rode with me to Portland, Oregon. I might say that the names of Andrew Cramer and June Dunning are merely fictitious as far as I know.

Note: In reference to Marion's body just before I delivered the portion to her father, I used a large needle which I had in my possession and some black thread to fix and hold the upper lids of her eyes open so that her father would think that she was alive when he saw the face.

The shirt with the name Gerber written on the collar which was torn and used to tie parts of the body of Marion was a shirt I had had in my possession since I left Kansas City in October, and which was given to me by my younger brother, Alfred. The name Gerber, I believe, is one of my brother's friends with whom he has traveled, and got on the shirt when it was sent to this man's laundry.

This statement is true and made freely and voluntarily by me.

William Edward Hickman

• • •

Even before William Edward Hickman completed his train ride to Los Angeles, the national media was reporting his obsession with the cinema. Coming in the wake of the theater fire in Canada, the men and women who were intent on building a major industry out of films were concerned about the connection the media was making between films and criminal behavior.

Three years earlier Louis B. Mayer had founded Metro-Goldwyn-Mayer and created what is commonly referred to as the studio system for making movies. He signed a limited number of actors and filmmakers and produced a steady stream of movies, with an emphasis on musicals and comedies. It was an impressive accomplishment for a young Russian immigrant who had quit school at twelve to support his family. His career in entertainment started with a vaudeville theater, leading to a move to Los Angeles and a partnership with Irving Thalberg. Together they made movies based on family values, high moral standards, and patriotism. They deliberately created an idealized vision of the world in the hope that the vision would provide a positive form of escapism from the challenges of real life.

From the beginning of his involvement in films Louis B. Mayer was concerned about the image of Hollywood, the image of the stars who worked for him, and the content of the movies he produced. Less than a year before the death of Marion Parker, in an effort to promote this image, he created the Academy of Motion Picture Arts and Sciences and set up the Academy Awards ceremony to honor the industry.

Louis B. Mayer was extremely concerned about the media frenzy surrounding the Marion Parker kidnapping. He read the newspapers and knew several newsreel teams from MGM had covered Hickman's capture and his extradition back to Los Angeles. He was also made aware of Mr. Hickman's inflammatory statement regarding his love of motion pictures and his daily attendance at theaters even on the day of the famous kidnapping and on the day of the hideous murder. Mr. Mayer understood better than most what negative publicity could mean for the movie industry. Canadians were advocating a law that would make it illegal for children to enter a film theater unaccompanied by an adult. The killing of an innocent child and the part movies played in Hickman's life could cost American studios millions of dollars each year if the subject was not dealt with properly.

Some of the negative publicity related to the Hickman case was created by the film industry. The relatively new medium of newsreels included images of the mutilated body of Marion Parker as part of their coverage of the Hickman case. Those images did not blend well with the wholesome style of entertainment Mayer was trying to provide. To complicate the situation, some theater owners were refusing to screen newsreels that included footage of the Hickman case.

Mayer understood the public concern and he believed the refusal to show the clips was a form of censorship, which

Mayer and the other studio executives would not tolerate. The studio executives set aside their competitive differences and made sure all the legal minds in Hollywood were prepared for the inevitable onslaught of government censorship. Clearly based on advice from his legal and promotional staff, Louis B. Mayer refused to make any comment on the Hickman trial despite repeated inquiries from reporters. His strategy was to take the moral high ground while working behind the scenes to counter the negative feedback created by the revelation of Hickman's fascination with movies.

There was another concern that remained unspoken in public. The introduction of sound to the filmmaking process meant pictures could potentially tell sophisticated stories with adult themes. No one knew for certain if this latent potential would be a boon to the industry or destroy the market. Unwanted negative publicity would simply confuse the issue. Any suggestion that films influenced behavior would and could encourage criminal conduct would ensure public support for censorship. In private, Louis B. Mayer made it clear he was not going to let that happen.

• • •

William Edward Hickman finished his description of his motives while still on the train to Los Angeles. Asa Keyes, Chief Cline, Chief Davis, and Detectives Lucas and Raymond read the newly signed document:

> My name is William Edward Hickman and this statement was made and witnessed on the S.P. Train en route to Los Angeles.

This statement regards the kidnapping and murder of Marion Parker. The time of the murder was Saturday morning December 17th 1927. The place was in room 315 of the Bellevue Arms Apts. in Los Angeles:

I wish to explain in full the motives which prompted me to commit this crime.

In the first place let me say that the only circumstances connecting my intentions of murder to Marion Parker are purely incidental. I was not prompted by revenge in the killing of Marion Parker. Only through my association with Mr. P. M. Parker at the First National Bank while I worked there as a page from January to June, 1927, made it possible for me to see Marion Parker and to know that she was P. M. Parker's daughter. This was an incidental due and I merely picked it up and followed it through. My motives in the murder of Marion Parker are as follows:

1. Fear of detection by the police and the belief that to kill and dissect the body I would be able to evade suspicion and arrest. I had warned Mr. Parker to keep the case secret and private but this he was not reasonably able to do so that the great publicity and search which followed caused me to use what I considered the greatest precautions in protecting myself.

After successfully dodging the authorities for two days I was overcome by such fear that I did not hesitate even to murder to escape notice. I consider that this fear and precaution were the result of my instinct for self-protection in time of danger.

2. Marion had a strong confidence in me for her own safety and I considered her own wish to return to her father Saturday morning too deeply. However, my desire to secure the money and return to college

were even greater. I knew that if I refused to take her back Saturday morning she might distrust me enough to give some sign which would cause my discovery. Yet I felt that if I did take her back in daylight I might fall in a trap and be caught. So in order to go through with my plans enough to get the money and keep Marion from ever knowing while she was alive that I would disappoint her confidence in me, I killed her so suddenly and unexpectedly, or she passed beyond consciousness so quickly and unexpectedly that she never had a fear or thought of her own death. Then in order to get her out of my apartment without notice I prompted after she was beyond consciousness to dissect her body.

3. For several years I have had a peculiar complex. Even though my habits have always been clean and although my high school record is commendable I have had an uncontrollable desire to commit a great crime.

This peculiar feeling, and I believe that it borders on the edge of insanity or that it comes as a weird relief from seriousness or deep thought, found a means of expressing itself in the Parker case, I am very sensitive and have a strong sense of pride. I have not been able to find a real practice value in religion or enough satisfaction that it is based on absolute reason. My deep thought on this subject and my apparent disappointment with my conclusion have shaken my sense of morality. However, I do not believe that I am insane or crazy, yet I do think that this complex of mine should be considered least among my motives in this crime. The fact that a young man is willing to commit crime to secure expenses through college and especially to a church school helps to explain this complex of mine. I cannot understand it myself but I do consider it a big motive in this crime.

I do not consider crime seriously enough. I think that if I want something no matter what means I have to secure it, I am justified in getting it. My record of crime illustrates this statement very thoroughly. Even in the matter of Marion Parker I could not realize the terrible guilt: I felt that some kind of Providence was guiding me and protecting me in this whole case. These facts, I believe, are associated with my complex.

I want to make a statement here to avoid any suspicion that during my connection with Marion Parker I took any advantage of her femininity. I can only give my word that I did not, but I gave this very sincerely and truthfully. My word is substantiated by the doctor's examination of the girl's body and I feel that everyone can be assured that the girl was not molested in any way.

I would like to say that I have had no bad personal habits. I have never been drunk or taken any intoxicating drinks. I do not gamble. I have never been in any corrupt conduct with the female sex. In support of these statements reference can be made to my record in the juvenile court of Los Angeles.

In giving these motives I have been as honest as I know how. I have searched my mind and impulses under all the circumstances and this is my truthful summary.

William Edward Hickman

As the train carrying Marion Parker's confessed murderer made its way south, it stopped at every major city, allowing newspapers reporters and the public to gaze at what the media called the "vehicle of justice" en route to its final destination.

After Mr. Keyes read the document describing

Hickman's motives he retired to a private room with a bottle of illegal alcohol. On the few occasions he came out of his compartment he was in no condition to make a public statement.

Chief Davis realized the physical condition of the district attorney would not play out well on the emotionally charged streets of Los Angeles. James Davis had been appointed chief of police little more than a year before the train ride to Oregon. After repeated allegations of corruption in the LAPD, Davis was creating an image for himself as the defender of law and order. His first reform as the new chief had been to create a fifty-man pistol squad he trained to become expert marksman. In a press conference he described the new unity by saying that "the gun-toting element and the rum smugglers are going to learn that murder and gun-toting are most inimical to their best interests. I want them brought in dead not alive and will reprimand any officer who shows the least mercy to a criminal."

Chief Davis knew that his announced intention to rid the city of Los Angeles of the menace of gun-toting rum smugglers would not be enhanced by the appearance of an inebriated district attorney. To compound his concerns, he received word from one of his assistants describing the main train terminal in downtown Los Angeles as being filled with four thousand people, all gathered in the hope of getting a look at the prisoner. Davis feared the large crowd could easily become unruly and make an effort to take justice into their own hands. He sent a telegram back to his department asking for a security detail of five hundred police officers to meet the train outside the city limits. He would intentionally disappoint the news media as well as the public by bringing

Hickman to the county jail by motorcade using back streets and alleyways.

It was an uncharacteristic move for the chief, who had a well-deserved reputation for self-aggrandizing behavior. Originally from Texas, Chief Davis liked to think of himself as being a vestige of the Old West. He had taken the best marksmen from his pistol squad and formed a pistol team, which travelled around the world demonstrating the shooting skills of officers on the LAPD. His favorite demonstration was to have officers shoot cigarettes out of his mouth.

Asa Keyes objected to the change in plans because he wanted the opportunity to impress the media with his quick resolution of a heinous crime. But the district attorney was in no shape to press the issue, and the chief prevailed.

• • •

In Kansas, after several days of uncertainty, Mrs. Hickman began looking for a lawyer to represent her son. Her first choice was the "Great Defender" Clarence Darrow, who had been involved in over fifty murder cases. He refused her request because he claimed he was already committed to several other ongoing cases. What he failed to tell Mrs. Hickman was that he was no longer able to practice law in Los Angeles, because he had been caught trying to bribe a jury and was disbarred from practicing law in California. Mr. Darrow did take the time to listen to Mrs. Hickman's story, however, and made a recommendation. He suggested that Jerome K. Walsh could devote the time to her son's defense that it needed. Mrs. Hickman, a divorced woman with limited financial resources, had the additional challenge of being mentally unstable. Without much discussion, she agreed to the appointment of Mr. Walsh as her son's lawyer. This step would not only give her son competent legal representation but also relieved her of the burden of being the only person speaking on her son's behalf.

Darrow left the meeting, instructing Mrs. Hickman to make no further comments to the media. She knew her silence would not stop others from speaking to the press, but was relieved she would no longer have to come to her son's defense. Friends of the family, neighbors, and old schoolmates expressed shock at the news that William Edward Hickman was a suspect in the case. Those who knew him claimed he was a charming young man, sometimes strange, maybe even a little weird, but not a killer.

Walsh was an up-and-coming attorney from Kansas who had been mentored by Darrow. Both men shared a moral aversion to the death penalty, which was the main reason Darrow made the recommendation. Walsh had recently gotten engaged and was concerned a lengthy out-of-state trial would be a strain on his new relationship, but his commitment to opposing the death penalty was strong enough to overcome his concerns, and he agreed to take the case.

During their initial meeting, Walsh told Mrs. Hickman not to believe what was being said. He also gave her no false sense of hope. His job was next to impossible and he knew it. To defend a confessed murderer of a child under normal circumstances was difficult, but when the victim was badly mutilated, when the case was as well-publicized as this one, when the suspect had given a number of confessions, the options for an effective defense were limited. For Walsh the first order of business was to find a lawyer in Los Angeles who could help him navigate the ins and outs of California law.

Jerome Walsh knew the average lawyer would not want his name associated with such a vicious crime, and he was right. After several false starts, he finally met and convinced a young lawyer named Richard H. Cantillon to accept the challenge. Cantillon was a competent attorney, who was unconcerned about public sentiment because he had earned his reputation as a lawyer defending high-profile gangsters in the Los Angeles area. Together they only had a few weeks to analyze, organize, and prepare for a trial of extreme complexity. They needed to address hundreds of legal questions while developing a reasonable line of defense for their client.

The initial legal maneuver was to address the legality of Hickman's three confessions: the one given by Mr. Hickman to his jailer in Pendleton, Oregon, the second confession given to the newspaper reporter for the *Eastern Oregonian*, and the third, formal confession dictated to the district attorney on the train en route to Los Angeles from Pendleton, Oregon.

After reviewing their legal options the two lawyers concluded that, despite some procedural issues, they would more than likely be unsuccessful in having the confessions removed from the record. They read all three confessions with interest, hoping to find something that would help their case. The one issue, which struck Jerome Walsh as odd, was Hickman's behavior just after the kidnapping, when he had taken the frightened victim to the movies at the Rialto Theater in South Pasadena. Walsh was unable to understand why Mr. Hickman would risk capture by taking Marion Parker to a public place, where all she had to do was scream for help. After discussing it with several lawyers and medical doctors, he came to the conclusion it was the action of an insane individual, who held the police in disdain and did not believe they could catch him regardless of what he did. This became the central issue for the defense: was their client insane at the time of the kidnapping?

The biggest legal hurdle the attorneys faced was Mr. Hickman's remarkable confession to the district attorney. To their dismay the confession dealt bluntly with the motives behind his bizarre behavior. His attempt at eloquence was compelling—as well as legal suicide. Mr. Hickman simply could not grasp the basic concept of the right to remain silent. Walsh believed the need to brag about what he did was further proof of mental instability.

At the first meeting they had with their client, both attorneys admonished Hickman not to discuss the case with anyone. Walsh repeated the warning, unconvinced his client understood the implications of failing to follow the instructions. Walsh's concerns proved to be well-founded.

While awaiting trial Mr. Hickman wrote a short note to another prisoner inside the Los Angeles jail. Before he could deliver it, one of his guards intercepted it and turned it over to the district attorney's office. It was a legal nightmare for Hickman's lawyers. The note read:

> Listen Dale, I believe you and believe I can trust you. Give me your advice on which one of these plans would be better. All the depositions aren't enough to prove me insane. I've got to throw a fit in court and I intend to throw a laughing, screaming, diving act before

the prosecution finishes their case, maybe in front of old man Parker himself.

Then to bewilder the jury, before the case is ended, I'll get up and ask the judge if I can say something without my attorney butting in. Then I'll get up and give all that crap about me wanting to do some good by living.

I intend to rap Mr. Keyes before the thing's over and pull some trick on him in the crazy line.

Shorty, think these things over and tell me whether it is best or not.

See you in the morning.

William Edward Hickman alias
The Fox Ha! Ha! Ha!

P.S. You know and I know that I'm not insane however.

The legal issue of insanity would now have to be supported by the idea that pretending to be insane is a symptom of insanity. There was some medical support for this notion, but it was going to be an extremely hard sell to any jury. It was a major setback for the defense, but Walsh and Cantillon felt they had no other options; the insanity plea remained their defense.

On January 25, less than a month after being captured, William Edward Hickman was brought into a courtroom on the eighth floor of the Los Angeles Hall of Justice. The room's decor was austere. The walls of the room were painted white with no pictures and only a black clock hanging above the entrance. Both the defense and the prosecution sat at one long table with about seventy-five seats behind them for the public to view the proceedings. At the time smoking was allowed in the courtroom, so the table for the attorneys was lined with ashtrays. Smoke lingered in the room due to lack of ventilation. The coffee cups next to the ashtrays smelled like rum.

Mr. Hickman and his two lawyers sat on the left directly facing the judge on the bench, with a witness box on one side and the jury seated on the other. The three windows in the courtroom were covered and the only light in the room came from half a dozen overhead fixtures. Spectators in the room were sweating profusely.

The courtroom was filled the first day, as it would be every day for the duration of the trial. The corridor outside held the overflow of concerned citizens wanting to catch a glimpse of the proceedings. At nine o'clock on the first day, all conversation in the room stopped as everyone watched the accused murderer enter the room for the first time. The guards escorted him to a seat between Jerry Walsh and Richard Cantillon. William Edward Hickman appeared relaxed, as if he were not aware of the reason he was in the room.

During the previous thirty days Mr. Hickman's life had been one continuous interrogation, with interviews by at least ten different psychiatrists, two lawyers from the DA's office, and two detectives from the LAPD. Besides this steady stream of government officials, Mr. Hickman had numerous conversations with his own defense attorneys, several newspapermen, and two ministers. For the defendant the change in his daily routine came as a relief. He wanted to have his day in court and was confident he would be vindicated. In his mind blame for the killing of Marion Parker belonged to her father, who had refused to follow his instructions. Once the trial was over he could return to his daily routine of watching movies.

Judge Hardy entered the room from a side door, the court bailiff's gavel hit his desk, and the noise reverberated against the walls of the courtroom. From the bailiff came the call to order.

"Please stand and face the flag of your country. Recognizing the principle of justice for all, for which it stands, department twenty-four of the Superior Court of the State of California in and for the county of Los Angeles is now in session, the Honorable Carlos S. Hardy, judge, presiding. Be seated please!"

Judge Hardy was the same judge who had sentenced Hickman a year earlier for the crime of forgery. This fact was not overlooked by the young defense attorneys. The judge nodded his head, ordering Mr. Hickman to stand while the court clerk read the indictment into the record.

In the Superior Court of the State of California in and for the County of Los Angeles. Indictment Number 32543 filed December 22, 1927. The people of the State of California, Plaintiff, versus William Edward Hickman, Defendant. The said William Edward Hickman is accused by the Grand Jury of the County of Los Angeles with the crime of murder, a felony, committed at and in the County of Los Angeles, State of California, and before the findings of this indictment as follows to wit: That the said William Edward Hickman, on or about the 17th day of December 1927, at and in the County of Los Angeles, State of California, did willfully, unlawfully and feloniously, and with malice aforethought, kill and murder one Marion

Parker, a human being, contrary to form, force and effect of the statute in such case made and provided and against the peace and dignity of the People of the State of California.

Judge Hardy asked both sides in a perfunctory manner if they were ready to proceed. Asa Keyes announced in a strong and self-confident voice, "We are ready for the People of the State of California."

No less confidently, the lead defense lawyer Jerry Walsh stood and faced the judge to make a point of law: "On behalf of the defendant, William Edward Hickman, I am filing a petition for the disqualification of Your Honor as trial judge in this case. I herewith deliver to the district attorney a copy of that petition, and hand the original to the court clerk requesting that it be filed in the records of this case."

The judge was not amused. Several reporters wrote that the judge appeared to be stunned, as flashbulbs popped from the back of the courtroom and reporters started scribbling in their notebooks. This last-minute legal maneuver caught both the judge and the district attorney off guard.

Judge Hardy addressed Mr. Walsh in an unfriendly tone: "On what ground is your petition based, Mr. Walsh?"

Refusing to be intimidated, Mr. Walsh responded: "On the grounds of actual bias."

Unknown to Judge Hardy, Ray Nazarro, Richard Cantillon's law clerk, had heard from a friend that Judge Hardy had spoken at a dinner party expressing his belief that Hickman's defense team did not have a chance of convincing a jury Hickman was insane. The judge went on to tell the gathering it would only take a few days to convict Hickman and then he would personally sentence the murderer to death by hanging. The judge took the next few minutes to read the petition, which gave other detailed examples of bias relating to the judge's behavior in pretrial motions. Without taking this motion under formal advisement, Judge Hardy responded after he had finished reading the last word. "Let the record show that I have read the petition for my disqualification filed on behalf of the defendant," he said. "In answer to the petition I, as judge, declare I would not sit in this case if I were of such a biased mind and entertained such prejudice that I would not extend to this defendant the full measure of his rights under the law and grant him a fair trial. Accordingly, I deny generally and specifically all the material allegations of this petition."

Mr. Walsh stood up once more and addressed the judge: "It is the contention of the defense that if this court persists in passing on its own qualifications, it will be denying this defendant a substantial right, that is, the right to have the question of this court fairness determined by an outside judge."

Deputy District Attorney Mr. Murray clearly saw the significance of the petition. He did not believe the defense lawyers would risk the wrath of Judge Hardy unless they knew something substantial. Fearing a mistrial, he asked for a recess, and the judge granted him thirty minutes. During the break Asa Keyes, Mr. Murray, Mr. Walsh, and Judge Hardy met behind closed doors to discuss the issue.

Judge Hardy returned to the courtroom and made the following declaration: "I have acquainted myself with the law upon which the defense is relying. I reiterate my statement that I do not entertain such prejudice or bias against this defendant as would preclude me from granting him the full measure of his legal rights and a fair and impartial trial. But rather than have this trial delayed by a court determination of the question of fairness as a judge and possibly prolonged by an appeal on that issue, I herewith present to the clerk my formal consent that this case be tried before another judge. This court will stand adjourned until ten o'clock tomorrow, at which time some other jurist will take my place."

District Attorney Keyes regarded Mr. Walsh, seated at the table next to him, with newfound respect and with the understanding that the trial was not going to be as easy as he had originally thought. The gentlemen of the press had their first headline. William Edward Hickman appeared to have no idea what was going on and had no apparent reaction to the ruling. His attorneys were elated.

The lawyers for the defense knew this was only one small victory and they had no legal alternative but to base their entire defense on an English point of law, one that had come to prominence after an incident in England in the 1840s. The principle of law was known as the McNaughton Defense, and took its name from a would-be assassin who tried to kill Queen Victoria. Mr. McNaughton was an assassin who was laboring under the illusion he was a member of a secret organization formed to bring about the destruction of the royal family. The court determined no such organization existed except in McNaughton's mind. Besides this major issue, the man made numerous delusional statements when he was brought before a British magistrate. At the conclusion of Mr. McNaughton's lengthy trial, he was acquitted of wrongdoing on the grounds that he couldn't understand the difference between right and wrong. The general public throughout Britain responded to the court's ruling with disbelief and disdain. Questions were raised in the media, seeking answers to how someone could commit such a serious crime against the queen and escape punishment.

The ruling was eighty-seven years old at the time of the Hickman trial. The precedent in the McNaughton ruling was established when psychiatry was in its infancy, and the medical profession had no clear definition of mental illness that could be used as the legal basis for arguing whether or not a suspect could tell the difference between right and wrong. Clarence Darrow had unsuccessfully argued that maladjustment was sufficient cause for claiming an insanity defense. Walsh was well aware of the failure and knew he needed a more persuasive argument. At the time the McNaughton ruling was established as law in England, extreme criminal behavior was considered to be the result of the influence of the devil. This meant the legal basis for the inability to distinguish between right and wrong was argued largely on a religious basis. The courts had since consistently ruled out the religious argument to the point that it was no longer admissible. This was in spite of the fact that, in 1927, a significant portion of the population believed mental illness was rooted in some form of demonic influence. Not surprisingly, the legal concept of insanity met with the same public disdain in California it had back in England in 1840.

As a student of Clarence Darrow, Walsh had studied recent developments in psychiatry. Originally the field had only dealt with extreme cases requiring commitment to mental institutions. Treatments were often brutal and arbitrary, more concerned with the care and maintenance of patents than any effort at finding a cure. This situation was radically changed by a neurologist named Sigmund Freud, who published a series of articles claiming less severe forms of mental illness had unconscious origins. Freud also claimed that unconscious mental disorders could result in physical symptoms. He developed a therapy called psychoanalysis in an effort to source unconscious influences that had a negative effect on mental health. Freud believed the primary source of negative unconscious influence was childhood sexual trauma. The efforts of Freud to establish his views as accepted medical theory were challenged by other doctors in the field, who disagreed with what they believed was his limited view of the sources of mental illness.

The formal legal ruling in California read in part:

> Has a party sufficient mental capacity to appreciate the character and quality of the act? Did he or she know and understand that it was a violation of the rights of another, and in itself wrong? If he or she had the capacity thus to appreciate the character and comprehend the possible or probable consequences of his or her act, and knew that if it was wrong, he or she is responsible to the law for the acts thus committed. And if not the burden of proof is on the accused; it is incumbent upon him or she to establish by a preponderance of evidence that he or she was insane at the time of committing the act charged.

The proof of Mr. Hickman's insanity rested solely with his lawyers; their mission was to solicit answers from their witnesses both in deposition and inside the courtroom, which would reveal the dark aspects of their client's sociopathic behavior. If the lawyers could accomplish this, the jury would begin to see a common element contributing to his increasingly bizarre and violent behavior. The problem for the defense was twofold. They needed to focus on one of many theories about the sources of mental illness, and then gather the evidence to support the theory. They had the additional problem of needing to gather the evidence in a month with limited resources.

Mr. Walsh spent almost the entire time before the trial traveling to the Midwest to take depositions from family members, friends, teachers, and Mr. Hickman's parole officer. His strategy was to reveal a criminal whose behavior went beyond the limits of a dysfunctional member of society. He wanted to show Mr. Hickman had been acting out a complete fantasy. He needed to show Hickman's reasoning was devoid of common sense. The risk was enormous. While the legal system was in the early stages of recognizing the significance of forensic psychology, it was still relatively new and was often misunderstood by an uneducated public. The medical arguments over the sources of mental illness were virtually unknown to the public. Any medical theory presented by the defense would be challenged by the prosecution. The sympathy of the jury would likely be with the prosecution.

The district attorney only needed to persuade the jury that Mr. Hickman had acted out of simple greed when he kidnapped Marion and killed her to protect himself from detection. The defense needed to persuade the jury that their client was incapable of forming the necessary intent to commit the crime. According to the defense, his inability to form the necessary intent was a result of insanity. Walsh and Cantillon were working with limited funds and could only afford to present one medical doctor and two psychologists to argue their side of the case, while the prosecution hired eight doctors, each well-compensated for their time and effort.

CHAPTER 4

"A wide screen just makes a bad film twice as bad."
Samuel Goldwyn

The city of Los Angeles, the Los Angeles Superior Court, and the district attorney escaped the embarrassment of a possible mistrial when Judge Hardy reluctantly recused himself from the case. The American legal premise of "equal treatment under the law" was settled amicably when Judge James Trabucco took his seat inside the courtroom on January 26, 1928. In assigning the unbiased Trabucco to the trial, the proceedings not only received the guidance of a distinguished public servant, it also received the experience of a renowned legal educator. At the time of his appointment, Judge Trabucco was considered one of the top experts on California criminal law in the state. He quickly reviewed the case, rescheduled the trial date, and completed the jury selection in only two days.

With a fully impaneled jury, the judge instructed the clerk to reread the indictment in the courtroom and for the first time announced the defendant's plea in a public proceeding. The clerk read the initial complaint without hesitation. He paused before reading from the second page of the indictment in anticipation of a reaction from spectators. The clerk continued reading in a firm voice: "The defendant Hickman pleads not guilty by reason of insanity to the charge, and is now here before you for trial."

There was a gasp of disbelief in the courtroom, followed by the shuffling of papers as reporters recorded the opening proceedings of the trial. The reporters were once again surprised by what happened in the courtroom when the judge addressed the jury and told them they were dismissed for the day. When the jury box was clear, Judge Trabucco addressed both teams of attorneys.

"Prior to September of 1927, when the new legislation went into effect, an issue of insanity was tried under the general plea of not guilty. Now, as I interpret the new law, that issue can only be raised by a special plea of not guilty by reason of insanity. A separate and distinct trial is required on this insanity issue. Gentlemen, I have spent all available time since this case was assigned to me searching for some precedent that might be of aid in construing these radical legislative changes. Frankly, I have found nothing of value. I will ask the counsel for the prosecution and the counsel for the defense if in their respective research they have discovered any guidepost that may help."

None of the lawyers offered to share any legal precedent relevant to the case because this was the first time a suspect had used the insanity plea in the state of California following the updated legislation. There literally was no precedent. The judge continued his effort to interpret the law based on his own understanding of the written statute.

"The record reflects that the defendant, Hickman, has entered the special plea of not guilty by reason of insanity. As I read this statute the defendant by such a plea is considered to have admitted the commission of the offense of which he is charged and seeks to avoid the legal consequences by the assertion that he was insane at the time the offense was committed.

"The law presumes all men to be sane. This evidentiary presumption places upon the defendant, Hickman, the burden of providing that, at the time of his killing of Marion Parker, he was insane. The defendant, having the affirmative of the issue, must go forward with the proof. It is now ordered by the court that you proceed accordingly."

With these few simple words, there was a radical shift in the way a murder trial based on the insanity defense would have to be presented in court. The judge was making case law, meaning he was explaining by way of interpretation the implication of the statutory or written law. This is always a risky venture in a high-profile case with public sentiment demanding justice for the accused. Anytime a judge offers a new opinion on case law, that opinion is subject to review on appeal. If the opinion is reversed by a higher court, it can potentially nullify the decision of the jury.

But Judge Trabucco had no choice, because the case was the first use of the insanity plea in a California court room following a recent legislative revision of the law. The insanity plea had been modified in California in reaction to the trial of Leopold and Loeb three years earlier. In the Leopold and

Loeb case, their attorney Clarence Darrow simply instructed his clients to plead guilty. The trial then proceeded directly into the sentencing phase. At the time, sentencing was at the sole discretion of the judge. Darrow's tactic was to present evidence of the maladjustment of his clients without the risk of a jury coming to a decision based on their emotional reaction to the brutality of the crime. Darrow also argued that maladjustment was an affirmative defense that mitigated the question of intent, without rising to the level of insanity.

The defendants Leopold and Loeb were two intelligent college students, both from wealthy and privileged homes, who murdered a fourteen-year-old boy for the admitted reason of proving they could do it without getting caught. Even though the plea was insanity, Darrow challenged the definition of mental illness and presented a case for the two defendants being misguided and dysfunctional. According to Darrow, Loeb had become maladjusted by losing himself in cowboy books and detective stories. Leopold was by his own admission in love with Loeb and willing to do anything he asked to please him. They started out by committing petty crimes and escalated to the idea of committing a murder without getting caught.

They then kidnapped Bobby Franks and demanded a ransom from his wealthy family. Workmen discovered the body before a ransom was paid, and Leopold was identified as a suspect when a pair of his glasses was found at the victim's shallow grave.

Darrow used four psychiatrists as expert witnesses to address the issue of maladjustment. The persecution objected to the testimony, because the plea was diminished capacity and not insanity. Darrow effectively argued that his clients were mentally ill but not insane. The public, the media, and the prosecution all reacted negatively to the distinction made by the famed lawyer. The judge ruled in favor of the medical evidence and sentenced the defendants to life in prison. Darrow claimed victory in the case because he had protected his clients from the death penalty.

California passed laws related to the insanity plea in reaction to the negative public reaction to the Leopold and Loeb trail. The case was still fresh in the public's memory at the time of the Hickman trial. It also presented a dilemma for the judge. California wanted to avoid the possibility of an accused murderer avoiding a jury trial. Unlike the Leopold and Loeb case, Hickman could not plead guilty to the crime and then introduce insanity as a mitigating factor during sentencing. In California the insanity plea could only be used in the context of a not guilty plea in the criminal phase of the trial. The intention of the legislature was to avoid the possibility of murder cases being resolved by a judge without the input of a jury. The California legislation was clear: the facts related to insanity needed to be presented to a jury. The legislature was also an attempt to eliminate Darrow's distinction between maladjustment and mental illness.

The problem for Judge Trabucco was that the California legislation was written in vague language requiring clarification from the bench. By pleading not guilty in the criminal charges, there was the necessity for a trial on the question of whether or not Hickman had actually committed the crime. Because it was impossible in California to plead guilty by reason of insanity, the procedural question was this: Could Hickman's lawyers present evidence of insanity during the criminal phase of the trial? The judge had indicated that the insanity issue could be part of the defense during the factual stage of the trial. He had also ruled the burden of proof for insanity was on the defense, and for that reason the defense would present their evidence first. This was a radical shift from courtroom procedure, which typically places the burden of proof on the district attorney. In most criminal cases, the district attorney presents evidence to support the charges. At the end of this presentation the defense has an opportunity to argue that the burden of proof was not met, and the judge is required to make a decision about whether or not there is sufficient cause to continue with the trial. If the trial continues, the defense presents rebuttal evidence. By allowing the defense to present their case first, Judge Trabucco was entering uncharted legal territory.

The judge went on to explain that California law allowed the defendant to plead insanity if he met the following criteria:

> The defendant has a partly sufficient mental capacity to appreciate the character and quality of the act. Did he or she know and understand that it was a violation of the rights of another, and in itself wrong? If he or she had the capacity thus to appreciate the character and comprehend the possible or probable consequences of his or her act, and knew that if it was wrong, he or she is responsible to the law for the acts thus committed. And if not the burden of proof is on the accused; it is incumbent upon he or she to establish by a preponderance of evidence that he or she was insane at the time of committing the act charged.

The defense team took full advantage of the change in procedure. They knew the district attorney would present the hard physical evidence of the crime, and that would easily prejudice the jury against an insanity plea if they felt the plea was a tactic to avoid taking responsibility for the crime. The strategy for the defense team was to manipulate the proceedings in their favor by introducing the most damning evidence before the prosecution had the chance.

The jury was brought back into the courtroom. Mr. Walsh wasted no time introducing a series of photographs taken by the police photographers of Marion Parker's disemboweled body. The audience and the jury reacted emotionally from the moment the first picture was introduced as evidence. Halfway into the collection of pictures one female member of the jury fainted, and Judge Trabucco brought the first day of the trial to an early end.

The next day, Mr. Walsh did the unpredictable once again by introducing Mr. Hickman's first confession given to Detectives Lucas and Raymond. He hoped to nullify the importance of the confession by entering it into the record as a defense exhibit. He was not overlooking the obvious; he knew that every word confirmed Hickman's role in Marion Parker's death, but he saw the legal maneuver as part of his overall effort to make the jury believe Hickman's behavior before and after the murder was so odd it fit the legal definition of insanity. He was effectively introducing all the potential prosecution issues into his defense of the crime itself. As Walsh introduced the evidence of his client's involvement in the crime he did so in way that focused on the apparent instability of Hickman's actions.

Walsh followed the introduction of the first confession by entering into evidence the second confession, the one Hickman had written by hand addressing his motives. It was not until the third day of the trial, after presenting several legal motions, that Mr. Walsh introduced the first witness for the defense. Mr. Hickman's father was called to address the issues of his family's poverty, the divorce of Hickman's parents at an early age, and the harsh religious practices of the family during Hickman's youth. Mr. Walsh was trying to generate sympathy for his client. It was a risky strategy, because he was essentially arguing that his client was driven insane by a strict implementation of Christian values. It was not an argument that would sit well with conservative jurors.

In addition to the testimony given by Mr. Hickman's father, the defense team added eleven depositions by individuals who had known Hickman in Kansas. All the statements were read into the record by the trial clerk in the hope the jury would see that Mr. Hickman was hopelessly insane. In the days that followed, Walsh offered several additional depositions to support the theory that Hickman suffered from abnormal behavior in the later part of his senior year of high school. The point of all of these documents was that William Edward Hickman seemed to have an abnormal aversion to women. He was described as having avoided contact and conversation with his female classmates. By all accounts, Hickman had made little effort to hide his feelings about women.

Cantillon watched the jury as the depositions were read into the record. He came to the conclusion the jury was not paying attention. It was a bad sign. After starting off with a strong legal strategy, the defense was in trouble. Walsh spent the next several evenings making sure he was prepared to effectively present the evidence of the medical experts.

District Attorney Keyes made very few objections

to the depositions. His own experience had taught him juries were seldom impressed by sworn depositions. Mr. Keyes knew the real legal battle, the jostling for courtroom supremacy, would start when each side started questioning and cross-examining the opposing teams of doctors. The district attorney was initially surprised by the willingness of the defense team to introduce what would normally be considered evidence for the prosecution. It was a bold move by a competent attorney and, based on comments from the media, Keyes seemed to thrive on the challenge. The district attorney came to the conclusion that the defense's tactic was ineffective and he let them progress at their own pace.

Mr. Walsh started his questioning of expert witnesses with Dr. Fettes, who spoke for the defense about the defendant's general physical status.

Q. I assume you reached a conclusion after your physical examination of this boy. Would you kindly relate them, Doctor?

A. I concluded that the patient, Hickman, had suffered a disorder of his natural growth. His circulatory system is inadequate. His metabolism was low; blood pressure was low; specific gravity of urine low. He has dysfunction of his vasomotor system. He suffers from general glandular disturbance. He is afflicted with arthritis. He is absorbing considerable fecal infection. He has an inflammation of the brain covering known as *serous meningitis.*

Q. Doctor, is Hickman's physical condition characteristic of dementia praecox patients?

A. Yes, in such patients a doctor usually finds, as here, a wide range of bodily disorders. This boy's physical condition is very characteristic of that mental disease.

In the early days of psychiatry, dementia praecox was the clinical term used to describe patients who believed they were the victims of demonic possession. Carl Jung published the first detailed study of this condition, stating the delusion was associated with physical symptoms that reinforced the patient's belief their body was being manipulated by outside forces. Walsh was trying to argue that his client's Christian values had created the illusion that his criminal behavior was influenced by the devil. From the point of view of the defense, this illusion was self-evident proof of insanity.

The next expert witness for the defense was Dr. R. O. Shelton, a well-known psychologist. He was there to present his opinion that the accused kidnapper and murderer had been insane during the crime and every day since. His key testimony came when he was asked by the defense about the source of Hickman's hallucinations.

Q. Doctor, could you determine the inception and nature of the defendant's hallucinations?

A. In this particular case, this boy's feelings towards religion characterized the nature of his hallucinations. As to just when he crossed the line into actual psychosis is difficult to say.

Q. What was that?

A. It was religion. When this boy was very young he lived in Arkansas, in a rural community, where they had religious revival meetings. At these revival meetings they would shout, get up and tell spiritual experiences, and become ecstatic. The boy described them to me. This boy was not able to stand the resultant emotional strain because of his inherited instability. He was terrified by the thought of hell. Religion is succor to the soul, but to the little boy it became a fearsome thing. It aggravated the terror instilled by the mother's maniacal night maneuvers with hatchet and butcher knife. He went home and prayed for hours, pleading with God for mercy. With the advent of puberty and its accompanying pathological and psychological changes, it was no longer possible for this boy, with his inherited weakness, to withstand this great emotional strain. He created a fantastic world ruled by a God of his own imagination. This God took on the face and figure of a revivalist. He falsely believed that this God talked to him.

It was Walsh's intention to prove Hickman had fought his natural tendency to suffer from the symptoms of dementia praecox by harboring illusions he was chosen by God to become a minister. That he had the idea that God spoke directly to him in response to feelings he believed were influenced by the devil was, according to the defense, the internal conflict that led to Hickman's insanity.

At this point Keyes started to object to the expert witness. It seemed to the district attorney that Walsh was using a "the devil made me do it" defense that could only be described as laughable. The judge disagreed. Walsh was allowed to continue with the presentation of his evidence.

• • •

Louis B. Mayer was disturbed by the impact the Hickman trial was having on the filmmaking business. Theater owners were refusing to show newsreels on the case and religious groups were organizing boycotts; the fire in Canada made parents fear for the safety of their children when they went to the movies without adult supervision.

On the advice of his public relations staff, Mayer made the decision not to discuss the Hickman case in public. Despite numerous questions from the media about the trial and the impact of Hickman's obsession with the movies there is no recorded statement from Louis B. Mayer other than him repeating the words "no comment."

His strategy for dealing with the negative publicity was to promote the newly created Academy of Motion Pictures Arts and Sciences. At the time of the trial the academy was making plans for its second annual awards event.

When the academy was first created it was considered a trade association for actors, writers, and directors. Mayer's original push for the creation of the Academy of Motion Pictures Arts and Sciences was an attempt to try and convince its founding members to mold the organization into a body, which would arbitrate contract disputes between the studios and the main creative branches of film production. The idea was to create an organization for collective bargaining on behalf of the people who made the film industry possible. It was, in effect, a union set up and run by the management.

Every attempt by academy members to break free of Mr. Mayer's influence was met with unmitigated failure. On every committee and in every meeting held to discuss issues of importance, Mr. Mayer had his spies and his supporters ready to inform him about the proceedings, and identify those who were not voting in the best interest of MGM. To that end he controlled not only the selection of the original thirty-six founding members, but also chose who would represent the different divisions of the organization at the subcommittee level, because he knew most of the hard work would be done by the smaller groups.

There were only six actors chosen to be on the original board: Douglas Fairbanks Sr., the husband of Mary Pickford; Harold Lloyd, the famous comedian; Richard Barthelmess, an actor who, for whatever reason, failed to make the transition from silent films; Jack Holt, the character actor; Milton Sills, a bit part actor; and Mr. Mayer's close friend Conrad Nagel. The six directors chosen for membership had all done business with Mr. Mayer: Cecil B. de Mille, a close personal friend; John Stahl, who gained fame for making a series of melodramas; Raoul Walsh, who was a successful director; Frank Lloyd, a small time director who worked independently of any studio; and of course Fred Niblo, one of the founders of the academy and an employee of MGM. The six writers chosen to join the Academy were Joseph Farnham, Jeanie MacPherson, Bess Meredyth, Benjamin F. Glazer, Carey Wilson, and Frank Woods. In the area of movie technicians there were only three: Roy J. Pomeroy, J. Arthur Ball, and the art director for MGM, Cedric Gibbons.

The remaining fourteen members of the academy were all producers who got along with Mr. Mayer even though many worked at different studios: Harry and Jack Warner, the brothers who ran Warner Brother's studio; Joseph M. Schenck, the original partner and friend of Marcus Loew; Fred Beetson, Mr. Mayer's close associate and friend; Charles H. Christie, who was famous for developing comedies; Sid Grauman, the owner of a large theater chain; Jesse L. Lasky, one of the founders of Paramount and one time partner of Mr. Mayer; Milton E. Hoffman, also one of the founders of Paramount; and perhaps the least successful producer,

M. C. Lee. The remaining three were Louis B. Mayer and his second-in-command at MGM, Irving Thalberg, and the only female member of the board, Mary Pickford, who asked to join not as an actress but as a producer. The petite, blond actress known as "America's Sweetheart" was both smart and independent. She used these attributes along with her star status to thrive in a business full of men.

The thirty-six members chosen to be on the board were not as surprising as those who were left off—men and women like Samuel Goldwyn, Adolph Zukor, D. W. Griffith, W. W. Hodkinson, Gary Cooper, Gloria Swanson, Charlie Chaplin, and Buster Keaton. Al Jolson and Eddie Cantor were not even asked. It did not go unnoticed that those who were left off the list had at one time or another had substantial differences with the great and powerful Louis B. Mayer.

Initially, Mr. Mayer was not even concerned about all the gossip that circulated around town regarding his control over the academy. To him it was inconsequential; what he knew from his experience in Hollywood was that, to get any idea off the ground, you needed a strong leader who moved forward regardless of how others saw them.

To help get the new trade organization going, he turned many of the details over to two well-established lawyers in the film industry, Edwin Loeb and George W. Cohen. These same lawyers were responsible for the public image of the film industry whenever a public figure got into trouble with the law. In this capacity, both attorneys had a close relationship with Asa Keyes. The support of the film industry was at the heart of his plans for financial and political support during the next election.

While the trial of William Edward Hickman droned on, Mr. Mayer took a significant step toward achieving his main public relations objective. He hired George Stanley to cast a 24 karat gold–plated statue that would represent the "Award of Merit." It was decided the statues would be given once a year to one individual in each category of the filmmaking process. The statues would be given out during an awards ceremony hosted by the academy. The statue was of a knight standing with his sword point directed toward the base of a reel of film. The reel was evenly divided into five areas, one for each of the five branches of the academy: actors, directors, writers, producers, and technicians. The statue was the symbolic representation of Louis B. Mayer's intention to defend the reputation of the film industry against all efforts to denigrate it.

• • •

As Mr. Walsh continued his argument that Mr. Hickman had been insane even before the kidnapping of Marion, he introduced a statement made by his client inside the Los Angeles city jail. It read:

> Is the abolition of crime worthy of deep consideration? Is it worth more than one life? Is it of such a widespread or inconsiderable nature that to check its progress is believed impossible or undesirable by the American people? Do the American people really understand crime? Can a criminal help himself? Do prisons help sufficiently to cure criminals? Do modern criminal prevention methods avail the people of the U.S. of sufficient protection or reasonable security? Has

crime diminished or is it increasing? Are murders and atrocities becoming more ordinary and less repulsive to the American people or is crime blotting out itself or is it not? Do the American people think they have satisfactory protection and control of their properties and lives? Are these questions of vital importance to every American citizen? Do their answers determine the welfare of American society? Will the American people listen to me? Will you members of the jury and court reason with me?

Crime costs the U.S. much money and many lives each year. Crime threatens society. Crime hinders efficient government. Crime disturbs the peace, property rights, lives, welfare, even the destiny of the American people. Crime is increasing in the U.S. Crime has become astounding in the U.S. Crime must be studied more carefully and checked. If this U.S. wants to continue, if the American people want a satisfactory solution to this grave situation, they must reason most thoroughly with young criminals.

I want to appeal to your complete justice, to your soundest reason to every feeling and sense that you possess. I want to do a great good for you. I want this case solved with the greatest and most beneficial results to society. I love the American people. I respect the people of California. I forgive the members of the prosecution and admit that they have a good cause to prosecute me. I want to help in a way that no one else has ever helped you. A great Providence is urging me to do this. Don't look at Edward Hickman and think only E. H. Don't look at murder and say only death. Don't look at crime and say only terrible. Think first of the welfare of your homes, your community, your city, your state, your nation. Think of peace and prosperity. Think of adjustment. Think of understanding. Think of your future and your city's future, your success and your city's success. Think of destiny and forget fate. Believe in yourself and your fellow citizens for good. Consider society.

I want Los Angeles, California and the United States to benefit from this case. I want society to see my example and derive a great benefit. In me has originated the tendency towards crime and there is a possibility in me for adjustment. Crime has been generated in me. Young criminality has been demonstrated in me. Now which is better, that I hang by the neck until dead and let public opinion gradually go back to normalcy until the next disastrous atrocity or would it be more fitting to place me on a shelf for life in a penitentiary adding me to the list of Loebs and Leopolds? I say that either of these courses is very inconsistent with the proper reaction to the case. What does my life matter to the American people? What does my death matter to the American people? Can't you see that it only confuses the average mind to try to discern in this matter.

If I hang some people will be gratified and some disappointed. If I receive life imprisonment some people will protest while some will agree. In case would the proper solution be found. Would the law be completely fulfilled: have modern criminal methods been sufficient then in making your lives and properties more secure and in diminishing crime? Crime will not stop with my trial. This case is not the finis of crime. Loeb and Leopold were sentenced to life imprisonment. Snyder and Gray were sentenced to death for killing of Gray's husband. Remus was sentenced to the asylum.

Has there been a noticeable reaction for the prevention and demolition of crime throughout the U.S. as a result of these notable cases? They represent each important phase of the modern system of court justice and criminal law procedure. Are they separately of collectively sufficient to the modern demands for the protection and security of human rights and properties? Are homes, families, cities and states any safer or less involved in crime? To be frank and honest with you in my own belief, I think not so.

You do want to save your own lives, do you not? You do want your own rights and your own liberties to be secured and safeguarded, do you not? You do want to check crime, I know you do. Well, if you kill me, you will not be doing any more than has already been done while crime will keep up just the same as before. If you sentence me to life imprisonment, you will not be doing any more than has already been done while your rights and lives will be in the same and increasing danger as before. If you send me to the asylum for life, you will be following an example hitherto tried but which has not benefited you while crime continue just the same as before and is even increasing and even threatening you more and more as each day passes by.

I am not being selfish when I beg and plead with you to save your own lives and properties do you think I am? I am not being prompted by personal insight when I try to bring about a great public benefit to you and the whole of American society. If you think so and if you do not think so, let me make at this time, a complete and open statement to the court.

It matters not, as far as I am concerned, whether I live or die, only as it regards your own welfare. I have already pleaded guilty to the crime, but before I die I want to do a great good for my country and for humanity. I give myself completely over to the jurisdiction of this court and to the judgment of your jurymen. I ask that you will allow me to explain the great calling of Providence, a great Providence which I profoundly believe has brought me into this world which has guided and directed my ever action throughout my entire life and which will take me away from this life at the appointed time.

Allow me to stand here like a man and explain the whole truth and honesty of my life and to offer you the plea which this great Providence has given me to utter. From the time of my youth, I have felt the presence of a great guiding power. This power has manifested itself in me and has made me feel that I would become great. It has made me feel that I would become widely known and that my name would live in history. It has made me feel that I would live to an old age and accomplish a great good for my fellow countrymen and the world. This great presence and you may call it God if you wish, but I shall call Providence, which has been with me since the age of twelve. I have felt it and known all these great secrets from this early age, and I can prove to you that it is real and that there is a likelihood of this fulfillment of this great work, if you will listen and hear my explanation.

In my life, there has already been a great range of activity. Environments, subjections, manifestations and accomplishments, all of which have been in a definite pursuit of the guidance and protection of this great Providence. My experiences have been such that I have been made susceptible to crime, and who have turned away from society. In plain words life was intended by Providence to exemplify the tendency in modern youth to generate criminality, and the terrible atrocity of my deed with the subsequent wide of this case, are only steps in the plan of Providence to bring me before the world so that I could do the great good which has been confided in me by this same Providence, for the benefit of society and especially the safety and security of human rights and liberties here in the United States of America. Let me explain.

I was born in Arkansas State and before I was ten years of age my father deserted the family and my mother was placed in the custody of an insane asylum at Little Rock, Arkansas. I had a broken home, so you can see, but before I left the country I tried to accept God, and it then being my twelfth year, I received the first calling and feeling Providence. I came to the city with my remnant family and while there I got discouraged with religion and the church. Religion in the city didn't seem serious enough and I began to disbelieve in it and God somewhat. I attended high school and graduated with second highest honors and scholarship in Kansas City largest high school. There was always quarreling and fighting in my family. We were poor and I didn't have money to go to college and I didn't try hard to get it honestly. I had discouragements and thought I would get a job and work and not go back to school. I tried several jobs and couldn't remain with any of them. I became dissatisfied. My family could not understand me. I was disgusted and felt hurt unjustly. I met two boys who wanted to leave home and be crooks. I was perfectly willing to do this because no one cared for me. I was disappointed. I wouldn't work, so I left home and took to crime. I always felt apart from society. I didn't actually know of one real friend. I even threatened to kill my own mother. I hated my father because he left me and married another woman and had other children. In spite of the circumstances, I always felt the presen of this Providence. I believe I had the making of a genius. My shaken morality always brought me back to the idea of college and preparation for this great thing I felt I was surely intended to do before I die.

A companion and I came to California in a stolen car and committed burglaries on the way. On Christmas Eve night, 1926, we entered a Pharmacy in Los Angeles and in a shooting battle an innocent man was killed. Here I received a positive manifestation of Providence. An officer of the law within three feet of me and with his revolver directly aimed at my conspicuous body fired three shots and touched me not even once. This was a miracle. This great Providence had saved me and proved itself to me. We continued in crime for a while longer and then decided to go straight. I got a job and stayed with it a few months and fell to the lot of forging checks. I was caught but received probation and went back to Kansas City, Missouri. I got another job and tried to go straight again but only stayed with it several weeks and was led back to crime again. This was only the work of Providence. I was only doing what many other boys had done whatever got a right start in life susceptible to crime and unaccountable for their criminal deeds. I thought that the end justified the means. I didn't recognize right and wrong. I wanted to be alone in my next crimes and get enough money to go back to college. I roamed over the East in stolen cars, and the Providence led me to come to California and Los Angeles in particular on Thanksgiving Day of last year.

On December 15 last I abducted a little girl by the name of Marion Parker from the Mount Vernon School and held her for a ransom of $1,500, to be used to defray my college expenses at Park College at Parksville, Missouri. Here I thought Providence made a great manifestation to me. From the lips of Marion Parker herself, I received this amazing and positive proof of the presence of a great Providence which was using me for a great work. Marion Parker told me from her lips and with great honesty that I confess my crimes before this court, I speak the true words of little girl. Marion Parker told me that in the very week that preceded her kidnapping that she had dreamed of a strange man coming to the Mount Vernon School and taking her away in a car. Marion Parker further related that in dreams she had many times been kidnapped and that she always felt that some day she would be taken away from her home and family, in this way. Even the little girl freely told me that she believed the whole thing was intended and if there is a God in heaven, I ask that he will strike me down at this instant if I am in the least particular diverging from the absolute truth and honesty not only in this matter but in everything that I say here.

These matters are of great significance. There is a great Providence prompting me to reach each word of this declaration and this same power brought this declaration from my own mind and I believe it has brought me to live and do all these things.

The murder of Marion Parker and the horrible, terrible, simply awful mutilation of Marion Parker's helpless body, a separate deed from the kidnapping of Marion Parker, a distinct crime done in blood with a knife by my own hands on the morning of December 17, 1927, in the bathtub in Apartment No. 315 at the Bellevue Arms Apartment of Los Angeles, California, was not meant by me, Edward Hickman, but through me under the guidance and protection of, and as a duty to this great Providence for the great work which it has been calling me since the age of twelve to perform for the safety and security of human rights and liberties in the United States of American. Please listen to me further.

Gentlemen cannot assign any other possible motives for my crimes. I felt it my duty to perform for my Providence and the hideousness of the affair and its widespread publicity were not intended by me for my own benefit or satisfaction, but were the works of the powers of destiny. My escape from California, my positive identification through valuable clues which a criminal seldom leaves behind, my detection and arrest in far off Pendleton, Oregon, and the publicity surrounding my capture were all steps in this mighty plan. They only served to bring the incident before the nation and to foreign nations. The entire U.S. is aroused and interested in this affair. It is meant by Providence for you, the people of this court and the people of Los Angeles City and County to listen and reason with me and act in a way that will satisfy California and America that the best solution of criminal law and punishment in this case will be made possible. The American nation is even beginning to expect that out of this case will arise some great solution. The United States is ready for the example of California. In California's hands lies the opportunity and right to bring a sufficient verdict in this case. Now, members of this jury and court, and I wish that the entire population of this state and nation could hear me at this time, listen to my greatest reason. Listen to my inspired logic.

Here I stand before you. You see that I am here and you recognize me as William Edward Hickman, who calls himself the Fox. You hear my speech and in your minds only can you reason for yourself. I am on trial for kidnapping and murder. I have pleaded guilty by reason of insanity. The question for you to decide is whether I am sane or insane. I believe that I am best able to speak for myself and judge my own mind and to say and feel of my own true condition. A human being always reserves the right and ability, I believe, to feel and express the true condition of his soul and mind, and knows his innermost parts better than his coexistat. Your duty is to judge me, concerning a condition, which only I know the true status. Yet, only in your own minds can you judge me for yourself and American society.

I only say that, if I was insane or am insane at this moment, I believe it not and say that it is a marvelous genius straining to keep itself alive, a mighty genius striving under Providence.

Whatever I may be, I judge it not of myself alone but from the power in me and over me of this great Providence. Listen to me now for your own cause and feel securely in your own reasoning that my greatest desire is for your good and not of any consideration for my own life or death. The acts of crime which were done by my own hands cannot be held accountable in my own mind but were intended for me by another presence to show that in adverse abnormal American social environments today, there is a tendency for certain unfortunate American youth to become enemies of their own society and to be classified as criminals only because society does not understand them and they do not understand society. These disappointed, dissatisfied, careless young men are the most dangerous faction in the United States today. This army of young criminals is steadily increasing. It is the product of society's own degeneration and weaknesses and, unless the American people take certain precautions or undertake new preventions, personal rights, liberties and properties here in this country will be greatly endangered. This affair strikes at the very heart of the nation. It is of fundamental importance and should be of your deepest concern.

The entire nation is looking on and waiting for the outcome of this trial. I am in your hands and you can do with me whatever you wish, I ask it of you to make such a study and observation of me before you kill me which will help in a new definite way to combat the spread of crime in the United States. I plead with you to do this for the benefit it may be to California and America, or even humanity. I ask that you will allow me to cooperate with you fully because I feel destined to help you in this great cause. I am just an example of your own reckless modern youth, but I have the greatest vision that in this example you will be better able to search out the tendency for crime and find a new prevention which be of great value to American society. I have always loved my country and it trills my heart to hear the Star Spangled Banner, or to witness the stars and strips in parade. I have always felt that before I died I would do some great good and Providence tells me that this is about the time.

I place my body in your hands. You can sentence me to hang if you think it will pacify those who crave blood. Is there not too much blood shed already in this country without having more? Are not the American people beginning to have the same bloodthirsty impulses that the young desperadoes and criminals themselves have? What terrible end will there be to society if these savage tendencies are allowed to continue? Public opinion never has expressed the true sentiments of the American people. The American press is responsible for many grave errors in this case alone. The American press tries to educate the mob in riot and bloodshed. The American people should, and will, resent these dreadful policies.

Let me make my final plea for the welfare and peace of the peoples of California and America. It is eviden to you that your rights and safety are of first importance to you. I ask to help in the preservation and continuance of these rights. Please take me and work with me and let this great Providence work in me for your good. Robberies and murders and public atrocities are steadily increasing, not only here in Los Angeles but everywhere throughout this country. I plead with you to take me and try to discover the means of staying the hands of young American criminals.

Why America! America! My country and your country will always live. Nothing will bring the downfall of this great republic. There will always be a great mass of the people who understand and keep peace and prosperity among us. Don't think this plea will be easily forgotten. It concerns the preservation of the very fundamentals of manhood, which are the foundation of our republic. It is inevitable that the people will understand and appreciate this reasoning, because I am not reasoning out of my mind alone but I have been inspired and guided by a great supernatural power in bring this message to you. Because I am not pleading for myself for my life but for the American people and for the protection of their own property and lives. Because, in my own confinement, will the greatest benefit come to my country through me. If I live, everything in me of Providence will be exerted for your good. If I die, I hope that some day my country will hear from another youth who is destined and guided by Providence unto the same great work that I have wished to accomplish.

For your consideration, and to your interest, may this message and plea be dedicated. I trust that you will bear me out so that the great power over me can exert itself for great good for the American people and humanity.

William Edward Hickman

The statement was read by the clerk. Once again the defense attorneys noticed the lack of interest on the faces of the jury. Their client's reaction did not help. During each day of the trial, Hickman's overall demeanor remained subdued almost to the point of disinterest.

Following the introduction of this statement a reporter named Edgar Rice Burroughs wrote a long article in response to the insanity defense. In the article he referred to psychiatrists as alienists, which was the preferred term at the time. It is a reference to doctors who studied patients who were alienated from their true nature. The reporter is also known for his creation of the Tarzan books, which he was developing for MGM so that they could be made into movies. There is no evidence that he wrote the article under pressure from Louis B. Mayer, but it is clear the article reflects the perspective of many in Hollywood who were concerned about the impact of the trial on their chosen profession.

Burroughs completed his reporting duties with the flare of a fiction writer, presenting his opinion interwoven with facts. The following is an excerpt from his article printed on February 4, 1928, for the *Los Angeles Examiner*.

> Hickman did not leap from his cradle, seize a butcher knife and dismember an innocent little girl, and yet Hickman was a born murderer. If nothing had thwarted his ambition, if no obstacles had intervened to render the winning of an honorable goal difficult, Hickman would never have committed a murder, nor any other crime. To the instinctive criminal of his type, crime is merely a means to an end. It is not in itself the chief consideration, as it doubtless is in the diseased minds of the criminally insane.
>
> Hickman's case is analogous in many respects to that of a very famous English criminal case of the early part of the Nineteenth Century, Thomas Wainewright, well known in his time as an essayist, a man with a brilliant future, started on a career of forgery and murder for the sole purpose of obtaining funds to satisfy his cravings for a life of ease and luxury. This was his ambition. In another it might have been an ambition to go to college. What difference does that make?
>
> He murdered relatives who had befriended him in order that he might obtain their property. One was a beautiful and very healthy girl he had insured for ninety thousand dollars. Her he poisoned. He was a man of super-refinement who hated all vulgarities and sordid instincts. Yes, he was very much like Hickman and a commentator says of him: "Wainewright presents to

us a perfect picture of instinctive criminal in his most highly developed shape." But nowhere, in all that has been written of Wainewright, have I discovered any suggestion whatever that he did not know the difference between right and wrong.

The defense will show that Hickman is not normal. Of course he is not normal in the sense that you and I are normal, or think we are; but in another sense, he is normal, he is a normal instinctive criminal and as such he is a very real and terrible menace to all of us and should be destroyed, as all his kind should be destroyed with dignity, for ourselves, and dispatch for them— especially dispatch.

If our criminal laws are remodeled to harmonize with our blatant claims to rationality a considerable mass of presently admissible testimony which now wastes a great deal of our time and money will, happily, go into the discard. What in heck do we care if the accused has two gold teeth and sore tonsils, or cirrus meningitis, or dementia praecox or that he is a paranoid who is suffering with megalomania? Mussolini may, conceivably be suffering with a megalomania, but I doubt that he would consider it entirely social to cut up our baby sisters, nor, if he did, that we should agree with him. These alienists ought to get together if they want us to have a lot of confidence in them. One of them writes a book in which he tells about epilepsy, while his brother alienist, testifying for the same side, describes epilepsy as an archaic, discarded term born of ignorance.

These alienists are the comedy relief of an otherwise full drama and if they accomplish anything else in criminal trials it is to fix definitely in our minds, as a conviction, a suspicion of long standing, that the estimate of the value of a gored ox depends solely upon whose ox it is.... If I were not aware of the high standing and unimpeachable characters of many alienists I should be inclined to ascribe motives to their sworn testimony that might make me the defendant in a libel suit, but I really do believe them sincere, most of them; and so I am moved to ascribe, what otherwise might fall into the category of idiocy or knavery, to the fact that psychiatry is as far from being an exact science as is alchemy or astrology and as such, it has no place in jurisprudence under our existing criminal court procedure. Briefly, I believe that it can only tend to befuddle the minds of the jury and becloud the real issue.

CHAPTER 5

"The subject matter is too distasteful to be put
on a screen designed to entertain a family."
John Wayne

The factual question facing the jury in the Hickman trial
was not whether or not Mr. Hickman had committed the
crime. The issue was whether or not he had been mentally
competent during the planning and execution of the
kidnapping and murder. In simple terms, the jury needed
to determine if Mr. Hickman had known the difference
between right and wrong when he committed each act.

Over the course of the trial the defense lawyers
asked hundreds of questions of their doctors to solicit
favorable answers. The prosecution asked their doctors to
give evidence which seemed to support their position that
Mr. Hickman knew what he was doing when he murdered
Marion Parker. During the trial the conflict of perspectives

led to heated verbal exchanges between the attorneys. But under cross-examinations many successful agreements fell apart and came back to counter the effectiveness of the original question. The following questions and answers began when Hickman's lawyer, Mr. Walsh, asked Dr. R. O. Shelton a simple question:

> Q. Did you as a result of these examinations and observations that you made, come to any opinion with reference to his [Hickman's] mental condition?
>
> A. I did.
>
> Q. Will you kindly state to the jury, Doctor, what that opinion is?
>
> A. He is suffering from dementia praecox, one of the worst types of insanity. He has one of the worst forms of this type. It is the paranoia type with delusions of grandeur. It is technically known as megalomania. He is a megalomaniac.

In the cross-examination of Dr. Shelton, the district attorney turned this mostly positive presentation into a disaster with one short series of questions and answers. The *Los Angeles Times* called the aggressive cross-examination a classic example of destroying an expert witness by his own words. The exchange started when Mr. Keyes asked:

> Q. He [Hickman] is incurable?
>
> A. Incurable. No chance of getting well, only deterioration now.
>
> Q. Do you think, Doctor, if this boy had appeared before you and you were sitting on a lunacy board, that you would have diagnosed his case as you have before this jury and recommended that he be confined in an institution?

A. I would have sent him up in the first thirty minutes.

Q. Isn't it true that all cases of dementia praecox the patient is rather silly and childish?

A. No, it is not true.

Q. You were in the jail there and talked with the defendant for the purpose of trying to help him out of his trouble, weren't you?

A. No, sir, I went in the jail to make a diagnosis, and I aided the doctor or tried to aid your alienist. I got them in and introduced them, or one of them. No, sir.

Q. Isn't it true you stated a moment ago that in your opinion, this defendant developed his form of insanity when he was about twelve years of age?

A. That was the beginning of it. I don't know whether he was actually insane. That was the beginning of that autochthonous idea.

Q. What do you mean, Doctor, by the term "malingering"? How do you define the term?

A. Malingering?

Q. Yes.

A. Pretending.

Q. Pretending?

A. Simulation.

Q. Do you think that a patient who was malingering could deceive you?

A. Well, I do not believe a case of dementia praecox could. I would not say that I am infallible. I do not want.... We are all fallible. I don't know that I am in this court, but I believe I am here.

Q. You do not know you are here?

A. No, I believe I am in this courtroom, but I may be mistaken.

Q. Well, that is somewhat of a delusion, isn't it?

A. It might be.

Q. You have delusions yourself?

A. It might be that is a delusion.

Q. Don't you believe, Doctor, that you might have had some delusions with reference to your statement that this man has dementia praecox?

A. I do not believe so, but that is my opinion. That is my honest opinion after a close, careful examination.

Q. In line with your reasoning, you might be mistaken about that. You believe it, but it might not be true?

A. I might be mistaken about anything.

Q. What?

A. I might be mistaken about anything.

Q. Oh, I suppose, Doctor, I might question you here for two or three days, which I am not going to do, and you would still hold the same opinion that you believe the defendant to be suffering from dementia praecox. That is true isn't it?

A. Well, that is my opinion now. I don't know what it would be three days from now.

Q. You don't know what your opinion will be three days from now?

A. No.

Q. Well I guess that is all.

Later in the trial, the issue of Hickman's sex drive was discussed in several questions put to Dr. Skoog by Mr. Walsh. In this series the defense team managed to present their view unscathed:

Q. Doctor, in your psychiatric examination, did you question this defendant on the matter of sex?

A. Yes, Mr. Walsh, I did.

Q. Has sex any relevance in diagnosis of schizophrenia?

A. Yes, it does. The absence of sex drive is a condition that most of authorities on the subject of schizophrenia have mentioned as present in their male patients. It is recognized symptom of the disease. Schizophrenia in the male also ordinarily diminishes the subject's fertility.

Q. Doctor, is the defendant Hickman, in your opinion, lacking in sex drive?

A. In my considered opinion, he is.

Q. Will you state your reason or reasons for your opinion?

A. I first will allude to Hickman's written statement introduced by the witness, Police Inspector Longuevan. This was prepared by the defendant for the avowed purpose of explaining his motives for his killing of the girl. [Dr. Skoog read from his notes] "I have never been in any corrupt conduct with the female sex." This statement of Edward's, made voluntarily to the police inspector and others, seemed entirely out of place and indicated to me that the matter of sex, in some way, was preying upon his mind. You may also remember that in the same statement, he laid great stress on the fact that he "had not taken advantage of the little girl's femininity", to use the boy's own words. This was also an unsolicited statement. The authorities had not challenged or charged him with sexually violating the girl. My experience as a psychiatrist has taught me that it is characteristic of the male schizophrenic to seek credit for his virginal state, which is due entirely to an innate lack of sex drive. It is a defensive mental mechanism as I interpret it. They will not face reality and admit the lack of sex drive is a shortcoming. The schizophrenic patient insists on transforming this deficiency into an attribute. With this in mind, I questioned the defendant on the subject.

At this point Dr. Skoog requested from the judge permission to read from his notes where he questioned Mr. Hickman on the subject of sex desire. After a brief discussion, permission was granted by the court and Dr. Skoog read the following passage.

Q. Your high school teacher, the assistant principal, Mr. Laughlin, testified that you were very popular with both the girls and boys at the high school. Was that so?

A. Well I tried to be.

Q. Did you have a particular girl you went around with?

A. There was a girl on the school newspaper staff that I used to take to school dances and social affairs at the school.

Q. Were you in love with her?

A. No. I was not in love with anybody.

Q. Didn't sex mean anything to you?

A. I was so busy with my public speaking and other school activities, I had no time to think about girls.

Q. But you must have had a crush on some girl?

A. No, I didn't. I knew lots of nice girls.

Q. But what about the girl from the newspaper staff that you took to parties?

A. She was a nice girl, very intelligent and well-liked at the school, but I never had a crush on her. I did enjoy her company and I think she enjoyed mine. We often discussed politics. She was bright. I never had my arm around her except on the dance floor.

Q. Didn't you ever have a desire to have sexual relations with anyone of the opposite sex?

A. I was taught that such desires were a sin.

Q. Have you had any sexual experience at all?

A. I have had girls try to excite me sexually.

Q. What did they do?

A. Once I was working as an usher in a motion picture theater. It was near the end of the last show at night. There were not many people left in the theater. A girl who used to attend the theater very often was sitting in the back row all alone. She called me over and asked me to sit next to her and we could see the last part of the picture. I sat down. She put her hand on my leg very carelessly, like she didn't know what she was doing, and after a while she moved her hand up my leg.

Q. Did that excite you?

A. No, I couldn't figure out if she was accidentally doing it or on purpose.

Q. What did you do?

A. I didn't do anything. I just sat there, sort of puzzled.

Q. What did she do?

A. She put her arm around my neck and pulled my head over and kissed me, and with the other hand she unbuttoned my fly. Then I stood up, and she said, oh, please sit down. I want you. Why do you think I have been coming to the theater all summer? I love you.

Q. What did you do?

A. I buttoned my pants and went out in the lobby. She waited for me in front of the theater. I sneaked out a side door after closing time.

Dr. Skoog looked up from his notes.

He then graphically told of other sexual experiences. In all of them, the female was the aggressor. His reaction to each was revulsion, which I interpreted as originating in his sexual inadequacy. The boy was very frank in his discussion, as his answers indicated. He did not relish this discussion: there were times when he appeared agitated to the point of anger. The conclusion I reached was considering his age, the lack of sexual drive that is apparent in male schizophrenics was manifest by my examination of this boy. You must keep in mind that at his age, sex impulse reaches it highest peak in the life of a male.

At the end of Dr. Skoog's testimony, Mr. Walsh asked the doctor for his prognosis of Hickman overall mental state. He responded:

> To me prognosis means, what I forecast for the future of this patient and what I think of the prospects of his recovery. Basing my answer upon the nature and symptoms of this case, along with my own professional experience and my study of the authorities, I say that the patient can only be headed for a rapid dementia. With this process, his mind will function less and his grandiose delusion, which drove him to great scholastic attainment and then into the commission of a crime, will disappear. He may then slip into a catatonic state, characterized by fixed stupor. Death will rapidly follow.

Mr. Richard Cantillon asked Dr. Skoog to read part of an interview he had with Mr. Hickman hoping to show the jury the nefarious circumstances by which they could declare Mr. Hickman insane. This interview was read into the record in what many felt was the most dramatic moment in the trial.

> Q. When you severed little Marion's body, what did you do with the intestines?
> A. When I cut across her stomach they were hanging out, and I cut the ends off and wrapped them in a separate package.
> Q. Did the content leak out?

A. I think there was a little bit of juice, but I think I washed it out in the tub; not very much came out, no substance.

Q. Are you aware of what will happen to you if the jury returns an unfavorable verdict?

A. Yes, the police told me I would be hanged.

Q. Are you afraid of dying in that manner?

A. Well, dying isn't pleasant, but I have no fear of death. Everyone has to die.

Q. I know everyone has to die, but death by hanging, doesn't that frighten you?

A. No, sir. What difference does it make how I die? One way is just as good as another.

Q. Don't you believe you are too young to die?

A. If my Providence decides I should die while I am young that is predestination. There will be some great reason for it.

Q. Do you consider yourself a Christian?

A. No, sir.

Q. What are you then?

A. I have a power over me that is equal and which is more than God to anybody, but that nobody feels. They have something over them and they are satisfied and I am satisfied.

Q. I understand you wished to study for the ministry?

A. I read the Bible. I have a New Testament and I have read Matthew, Mark, Luke and John. This morning I read some of the Revelations. I do not care to read the Old Testament; I don't understand it, as it has not much in it for me.

Q. Is your reading of the New Testament in conformity with this Power you have over you?

A. Yes, I must know what is in it to preach.

Q. What is this Power you have over you?

A. It is a Divine Power. It is Providence.

Q. Then it is God?

A. No, it is superior to God; it is different; it does not work the same way.

Q. Does anyone other than yourself have the benefit of this power?

A. No, sir. It is especially for me.

Q. Why should you be different from others?

A. Well, I know I am different.

Q. How long have you felt different?

Q. Do you think you are crazy?

A. No I do not.

Q. But you just said you were crazy.

A. Crazy has lots of different meaning. I have had a lot of people call me crazy, but I do not believe they mean it.

Soon after completing the reading of this interview, Dr. Skoog was asked to relate another conversation he had with Hickman, hoping the jury members could see Hickman's defective thought process:

Q. Is what you told me a sacred secret?

A. Yes, sir. I seldom tell anybody.

Q. Are you directed to keep it secret?

A. I can tell you. I told my mother of it. I told my friend, Don Johnstone. I told Mr. Cantillon and Dr. Shelton because they must know to understand me. They are helping me. I told Mr. Moise who comes to visit me; he is writing a story about me. I never like to disclose my complete views on it; that is, in trying to explain it, I just haven't words to give the exact idea of it. It talks to me and suggests things. I hear it, I have seen it. Beyond any double, it really exists. It has been known to me for a long time. I do not try to overcome this power. It is far

greater than I am. I am humble, passive and obedient to
it. It is something I should not try to understand.

Q. Can you tell me more about how this Power makes
itself known to you?

A. I feel the Power over me. With the aid of the Power
I know I will become great. I never stop to figure it
out. If the Power directs me, I do it. I know it will
lead to a great end. I think it plans everything for
me. It is predestination. All human beings no matter
how smart they are have only a shade of concept of
the Universe. But the Power knows all. It is Supreme
Greatness. I used the name Providence but that does
not exactly describe it.

Q. Do you know of anyone else with whom your
Providence communicates?

A. It has not been revealed to anyone else, not even Christ.

Q. You say Providence talks to you; how does it sound?

A. It is soft, but powerful. When it is speaking, I cannot
move. Chills run down my spine.

Q. You have seen pictures of God in his white flowing
robes. I presume your Providence appears much
like God.

A. No, my Providence has fiery eyes; they seem to burn a
hole in me.

Mr. Cantillon then took his questioning in a different
direction, asking Dr. Skoog to discuss Hickman's religious
beliefs.

Q. Doctor, did the defendant, during your examination of
him, give you a reason why he killed Marion Parker?

A. Yes, he did. May I go on and explain?

Q. Yes Doctor, go right ahead.

A. I asked him why he killed the girl. He said he never

intended to harm her when he took her from her school. He abducted her for the sole purpose of obtaining $1,500.00 so he could attend Park College. Thank you. This is the defendant speaking: I think she was actually born and lived for this thing. It is true she may not then have known about it, but she was prepared and brought into this world for this very thing.

The defense rested their case unconvinced they had persuaded the jury. Walsh and Cantillon closed their case, went back to Cantillon's office, and reviewed their evidence in the hope they could find something they had missed.

• • •

With the first Oscar night under his belt, Louis B. Mayer made a list of items to improve the selection process and the ceremony scheduled for the following year. He now understood that his power in Hollywood was just beginning to be felt outside the wall of the MGM studio. He turned this newfound success to yet another issue he was passionate about. Mr. Mayer, more than any other studio chief in Hollywood, worried about the issue of censorship in the film industry. He was particularly upset over the refusal of some theaters to show the ongoing news clips about the progress of the Hickman trial.

The reasons behind his paranoia are not clear. Some of his biographers have suggested the issue had its beginning in an incident which took place in 1922 in the city of Pasadena, California. The local police chief and several of his officers had stopped MGM's first preview of the movie, *The Merry Widow*. Just as the plot in the film got to a scene where the leading man was holding the actress in a less-than-glamorous pose, the theater lights were turned on and the projector turned off by the local police. Authorities confronted Mr. Mayer and Mr. Thalberg, who were both in the audience.

It was reported that the city's police chief contemplated arresting the two men as the producers of an immoral film. Mr. Mayer spoke to the audience, praising their chief of police and the citizens of Pasadena for their high moral standards. He told them he appreciated their position and was not fully informed about the content of the film. He promised the audience and the police department he would take the film back to Hollywood, where he would personally have the director make the needed changes to the storyline to meet or exceed the prevailing standards of their community. He swore to everyone that the remake of the film would produce a story decent enough for the whole family to watch. He even went so far as to promise he would return for their approval in a matter of weeks.

Mr. Mayer kept his promise to the city of Pasadena, and the film went on to receive a huge amount of free press and in the process became one of MGM's most profitable films of the year, proving the Hollywood maxim that even bad publicity is good publicity. The event, however, remained with Mr. Mayer, and the fear that American audiences might one day revolt on moral grounds against the whole movie industry was always present in his mind.

The issue for Mayer was complex. On one hand he did not want to offend his audience. On the other hand he did not want to relinquish his personal control over the filmmaking process. He clearly did not want theater owners feeling they could dictate content.

The first attempt at censorship against the motion-picture industry in the United States came from the citizens of New York City. The New York Board of Motion Picture Censorship was first formed in 1909 because a group of women felt the movie industry was not the group that should set the bar on what was acceptable and what wasn't. The motion picture industry was still new, and so disorganized that the producers had no means to fight the forces trying to dictate the limits on their freedom of speech. The new board of censorship requested theater owners submit their films ahead of time for their seal of approval. Eventually every major studio agreed to have their finished product reviewed for suitable content before distribution in New York. If the board found something unsuitable, the studios went through the additional expense of making changes before releasing their films to theatre owners nationwide. Six years later, in 1915, the board's influence inside the industry increased to the point they changed its name to the "National Board of Review."

As much as the major studios disliked their actions being dictated in this manner, they understood the board actually helped the movie industry ward off congressional interference. Three bills were introduced to create a Federal Censorship Commission, a proposed federal agency that would have had the power to deny copyright to any film the members felt inappropriate for family viewing. Louis B. Mayer used all his political clout to defeat all three congressional bills. At the same time, he understood that the emotional issues behind the call for censorship guidelines could raise major problems if the quality and content of movies failed to conform to the perceived standard of common decency.

The newsreels covering the Hickman trial once again raised the issue of congressional intervention. Mr. Mayer, the businessman and the moralist, found himself caught in the middle of this nationwide struggle. Always the realist and diplomat, Mr. Mayer often took both sides of the issue when asked for an opinion. In response to the question, can having sexual content in a film help at the box office, he is quoted as saying: "You'd be surprised how tits figure in a hit movie." But when talking to Hedy Lamarr about her personal life, he responded quite differently. "If you like to make love, then screw your leading man in the dressing room, that is your business, but in front of the camera, gentility. You hear? Gentility!"

When Congress failed to pass nationwide laws governing a film's decency, many groups changed their tactics and went to the judicial branch of the government for legal recourse. There they won a significant legal case named "Mutual Film Corporation v. Ohio Industrial Commission." The judge in that case ruled that censorship was legal but left the issue of censorship to each individual state. Within a matter of two years, over 40 percent of American's population saw some form of censorship at the state level.

By 1922, the same year Mr. Mayer was confronted by the police chief of Pasadena, the movie industry found itself in a state of complete chaos. The expense of responding to each state's requirements over censorship was becoming astronomical in both logistics and re-editing costs. Mr. Mayer, with little support from other studio chiefs, made several unilateral decisions to bring the problematic situation to an end before it stymied the whole film industry. His answer to the problem was not unlike the one he had used to create the Academy of Motion Pictures Arts and Sciences. He called his new organization the "Motion Picture Producers and Distributors of America." His intention was to maintain control over the process of censorship by setting up an independent commissioner staffed with personnel he selected. The so-called independent commissioner just happened to be a very close friend of Louis B. Mayer's, William H. Hays. The commissioner was a former postmaster general, hired at the unbelievable salary of $150,000 a year to wrestle control of censorship away from outside groups and state governments. Hays performed admirably, consolidating the process and giving the impression of independence.

In 1927, just months before the Hickman trial, Hays introduced to the public the Association of Motion Pictures Producers and Distributors of America Code. It became more commonly known as just the "Hays Code." It read as follows:

> Resolved, that those things which are included in the following list shall not appear in pictures produced by the members of this Association, irrespective of the way in which they are treated:
>
> 1. Pointed profanity by either title or lips to include the words 'God,' 'Lord,' 'Jesus,' 'Christ,' (unless they are used reverently in connection with proper religious ceremonies), 'hell,' 'damn,' 'Gawd,' and every other profane and vulgar expression however it may be spelled.
> 2. Any licentious or suggestive nudity-in factor in silhouette; and any lecherous or licentious or

suggestive notice thereof by other characters in the picture.

3. The illegal traffic in drugs.
4. Any inference of sex perversion.
5. White slavery.
6. Miscegenation (sex relationship between the white and black race).
7. Sex hygiene and venereal diseases.
8. Scenes of actual childbirth-in fact or silhouette.
9. Children's sex organs.
10. Ridicule of the clergy.
11. Willful offense to any nation, race or creed.

These were the issues the association felt most strongly about, but there were still others they felt needed to be addressed. To compensate for the other issues, the following list of issues was added.

And be it further resolved, that special care be exercised in the manner in which the following subjects are treated, to the end that vulgarity and suggestiveness be eliminated and that good taste be emphasized:

1. The use of the Flag.
2. International relations (avoiding putting in pictures an unfavorable light of another country's religion, history, institutions, prominent people, and citizenry).
3. Arson.
4. The use of firearms.
5. Theft, robbery, safe-cracking, and dynamiting of trains, mines, building, etc. (having in mind the effect which a too-detailed description of these may have upon the moron.)
6. Brutality and possible gruesomeness.

7. Techniques of committing murder by whatever method.
8. Methods of smuggling.
9. Third degree methods.
10. Hangings or electrocutions as legal punishment for crimes.
11. Sympathy for crimes.
12. Attitude towards public characters or institutions.
13. Sedition.
14. Apparent cruelty to children and animals.
15. Branding of people or animals.
16. The sale of women, or of a woman selling her virtue.
17. Rape or attempted rape.
18. First-night scenes.
19. Man and woman in bed together.
20. Deliberate seduction of girls.
21. The institution of marriage.
22. Surgical operations.
23. The use of drugs.
24. Titles or scenes having to do with law enforcement or law-enforcing officers.
25. Excessive or lustful kissing, particularly when one character or the other is a heavy.

The response by writers, directors, and producers to these new rules was anything but favorable. They struggled to interpret exactly what the association meant by its "Don't and Be Careful" list. The failure of such a general approach to the artistic process became all too clear when it was realized there were no penalties imposed for violations to the code.

The whole issue of censorship and improving

Hollywood's image came to the forefront only after a series of scandals that rocked the motion-picture industry at the turn of the century. The three major scandals, which stood out among the many, were the Fatty Arbuckle trial for rape and manslaughter, the William Desmond Taylor murder mystery, and the drug-related death of Wallace Reid.

In the twenties Fatty Arbuckle was one of the highest-paid actors in Hollywood. He was tried for the rape and murder of Virginia Rappe. The prosecution's theory was that the victim had been crushed by Arbuckle while being raped. The jury found him not guilty, but he was clearly convicted in the court of public opinion and afterward disappeared from both Hollywood and filmmaking.

William Desmond Taylor was a popular director and actor during the silent film era. On February 2, 1922, he was found dead in his Los Angeles home. A doctor who examined the body claimed he had died of a stomach hemorrhage. When the police arrived they discovered a bullet wound in his back. No suspect was ever charged in the crime. The identity of the person responsible for the murder was a common source of speculation in the media for over year. Many years later reporter King Vidor said: "I interviewed a Los Angeles police detective, now retired, who had been assigned to the case immediately after the murder. He told me, 'We were doing all right and then, before the week was out, we got the word to lay off.'"

During the era of silent films, Wallace Reid was a popular leading man often described as "the screen's most perfect lover." He claimed to have become addicted to morphine as a result of painkillers needed because of injuries he received during a train wreck. He checked himself into a sanitarium in an effort to kick the addiction and died there. Following his death his wife Dorothy Davenport went on tour to publicize what at the time were the relatively unknown dangers of drug addiction. Her positive intentions backfired and fueled public suspicion that actors were overly indulgent.

In response to these scandals Louis B. Mayer hired a staff of lawyers whose job it was to protect the image of anyone involved in the film industry. Mayer and most of the other studio heads supported the reelection of Asa Keyes largely because he was willing to work with studio attorneys in a way that mitigated the possible damage of a potential scandal. In exchange for his support studio executives were known to make generous contributions to his campaign. Some reporters suspected the support went beyond political fundraising. Such rumors were never confirmed. But the support for Asa Keyes was at the heart of concern over the censorship of the Hickman newsreels. The trial was at the heart of Keyes's reelection strategy. To ignore the trial could be interpreted as giving support to those who were considering opposing Keyes in the upcoming election.

In Oklahoma and Kansas, theater owners were boycotting the newsreels reporting on the Hickman murder trial. They thought the subject was too gruesome for the general public. In the city of Ada, Oklahoma, the issue of censorship made the news when the mayor and the PTA requested the newsreel be removed from one of their local theaters. One of the theater owners refused to even consider the idea, and several public officials became outraged. The dispute went immediately to the courts, where the ban of the newsreel became a hot political issue. Mr. Mayer knew instinctively that the repercussions of the court ruling could go beyond this one case. The theater owner who wanted to show the newsreel lost his first legal battle in the local courts. He immediately appealed the decision to the appeals court, and lost again when it was ruled the ban was constitutional.

The decision was in fact keeping with the times. Unlike the standards in place for movies, there was no system to determine what was or was not acceptable behavior in newsreels. So local groups and politicians were arbitrarily banning or editing newsreels based on local standards of morality. One of the first cases went to court in 1908, a case in which the mayor of New York closed every movie house in the city when it was reported a few theaters were showing obscene material. A year later, a court ruling in Atlantic City closed theaters and physically removed the film *Dolorita in the Passion Dance* from Edison's Kinetoscopes when women complained to the mayor that scandalous behavior was emanating from the projection boxes.

What happened in Ada, Oklahoma was unanticipated by anyone in the film industry. The idea that real life could be so hideous that even newsreels would have to be censored in order to stop their contaminating influence on impressionable youth had been unthinkable. The decision in Oklahoma created a state of panic in Hollywood.

CHAPTER 6

"The movies we love and admire are to some extent
a function of who we are when we see them."
Mary Schmich

Asa Keyes was not impressed by the expert witnesses
presented by the defense. He believed the jury was equally
skeptical. His approach to cross-examination was to ridicule
the experts' conclusions and to clearly show his contempt
for their opinions in the way he asked his questions.

The defense's effort to label William Edward Hickman
as someone who suffered from dementia praecox was a
risky tactic, because the concept itself was not fully accepted
within the medical profession. It was generally described as
cognitive disintegration, usually starting in late childhood.
This disintegration generally involved loss of memory, and
the inability to act on goal-related behavior. The unpopularity
of the diagnosis was based on clinical observations that

associated the condition with the patient's belief they were possessed by spirits. The first in-depth study of dementia praecox was completed by Carl Jung as his doctoral thesis. In the study he explained as many symptoms as he could, but left the door open to the possibility of some type of external spirit influence. This aspect of the condition eventually led to the medical profession dismissing it as an acceptable diagnosis. Eventually the condition was relabeled as schizophrenia. During the Hickman trial, the medical profession was in the midst of a debate on the legitimacy of the condition as a true symptom of mental illness.

The district attorney presented eight expert witnesses who reflected his contempt for the diagnosis and who questioned the medical validity of the condition. Doctor after doctor appeared to reinforce what the jury was already feeling: the case for mental illness was based on Hickman's desperate attempt to avoid taking responsibility for his crimes.

As the trial approached its end, both sides prepared to give their closing arguments. The judge ruled the co-counsels would be allotted time for a summation of the case. Each lawyer would try and persuade the jury members of the evidentiary points that favored their side of the case.

Mr. Murray went first with his summation of the prosecution's case. He spoke methodically, introducing both facts and arguments that Asa Keyes could build on during his summation. Newspapers reported that the tall, handsome lawyer transfixed the jurors in a logical review of the testimony by summarizing the issues put forward by the state's key witnesses. The lawyer presented the prosecution's objections to the mental illness defense without sarcasm.

With his objective presentation, Mr. Murray set the stage for his boss to deliver a knockout punch emphasizing the emotional issues that were so abundant in the Hickman case. Mr. Walsh's presentation to the jury, on the other hand, was not well-received by the newspapermen in the audience. They saw his presentation as neither clear nor precise. He often used a conspicuous display of verbiage to make a simple point and he also spoke on issues of good and evil in such abstract, convoluted terms that many of the newspapermen in the audience found it impossible to summarize the ideas in their columns. He even misrepresented evidence, which could have backfired if the prosecution felt it had been necessary to object. Walsh claimed Mr. Hickman stayed in his apartment all day after he murdered Marion Parker, when the evidence showed he had gone out to mail the ransom notes and to watch a movie.

On the other hand, Mr. Cantillon had a commanding presence when he spoke to the court. He regaled the jury for over an hour with an overview of two weeks' of testimony. District Attorney Keyes sat back in his chair, watching and weighing the reactions of jury members to what was being said by the defense team.

> Now, as to the statement of the issue of this case, the issue, as you all understand it, is simply this: whether or not this defendant is sane or insane. There is nothing else in the case. It is an extremely difficult matter to adjudicate upon, I know, ladies and gentlemen of the jury, due to the fact that the machinations of the human mind and the vagaries of the human mind are things that are very difficult to trace, but regardless of how difficult it is, or how unscientific the investigation must be, it is

the only investigation that we have at present time; it is the only investigation that the law has given us; it is the only investigation that the legislature has provided for us; we must assume the burden here and now of determining whether or not the defendant, William Edward Hickman, at the time of the commission of these offenses alleged in the indictment, was sane or insane.

Now, the law is an inquisition relative to the sanity or insanity of the defendant, like the law in all of its other phases, attempts to be very correct. It attempts to draw a fine line; it attempts to set up a standard and a rule, and the rule that it has set up in this particular case is known as the "right and wrong test." It is a rule which has been invoked for two or three hundred years, and regardless of what criticisms may be placed upon it, no one has introduced and no one has suggested a rule which would be better in its application, so, consequently, regardless of what you or I or anybody else may think of the rule relative to the right and wrong test, it is the rule that is incumbent upon us to measure the sanity or insanity of this boy.

There is nothing about the rule itself that is difficult to understand. It is in the application of this particular rule that we find difficulty arises because, ladies and gentlemen of the jury, to follow the effect of disease upon the human mind is something that is extremely difficult for you or for me to trace and, from the evidence as it has been presented here, we know it is something that is extremely difficult for even men of science, who have devoted their entire lives to the subject, to trace with any certainty, so we enter upon this proposition and we discuss this evidence, and we consider it, and we must be just about it, and we must accord to the defendant the mercy, and only the mercy, that the law accords to him, and that is the right to a calm and impartial deliberation upon these facts to determine whether or not at the time this act was committed he knew the difference between right and wrong.

It is true that the burden of proof in this case is upon the defendant. He must prove by a preponderance of the evidence that at the time he committed these acts as charged in the indictment that he was an insane person. That rule places him in a position that, under any other plea known to the law the burden of proof is upon the state, but this has reversed the order of things, this new law which is the forerunner, possibly, of many changes to come, has reversed the order of things, and has placed the burden of proving his insanity upon the defendant himself. It is an extremely difficult thing sometimes to assume this burden of proof, due to the fact that the resources of a defendant certainly are not in any measure comparable with those of the state of California. It is an extremely difficult thing to carry this burden of proof and to establish it by a preponderance of evidence when there is no money, where there are no friends, when there is no assistance in the case.

After discussing the details of the law Cantillon went on to say:

I feel that if you follow that instruction there is only one conclusion that you can come to, there is only one reasonable conclusion that you can reach, there is only one consistent conclusion that you can reach, and that is that William Edward Hickman is insane.

Insanity is a strange, a peculiar thing. I don't know

how to define it. It is like many other workings of the
mind, it is difficult to define, because the organ that
attempts to define it is the one that is also attempting
to define its own condition; so it makes it an extremely
difficult thing to do; but there is a type of insanity, ladies
and gentlemen of the jury, that we have attempted to
establish here, a type of insanity that I think we are
absolutely justified in advancing here, and that is the type
of delusional insanity, where a delusion or a stimulation
of the imagination, either through mental stress or
thought the ravages of the diseased or imaginable
parts of the mind is so stimulated so as to cause the
imagination itself to create delusions that absolutely
control the mind and, through the mind, controls every
other organ of the body. That is a fine hairline between
and orderly mind and a deranged mind. One faculty
out of order, ladies and gentlemen of the jury, may
destroy and may disturb every other part of the mind,
so that a man, while he would have the remainder of
his faculties intact, would be so deranged that he could
not and would not, because of this controlling delusion,
understand the difference between right and wrong.

At this point in the closing argument the judge ordered
a recess. When the court session resumed, Cantillon argued
that William Edward Hickman inherited his insanity from
this grandmother who, fifteen years earlier, had been
committed to what was then known as a mental institution.
Cantillon used his client's grandmother's condition as the
basis for establishing the existence of mental illness in the
Hickman family.

Therefore, we have established the insanity of the
grandmother; we have established epilepsy in a first

cousin; we have conclusively established insanity in the mother; and you know the testimony about the grandfather and I do not intend to dwell on him a great deal. I do not think the man was insane, but I think he would come under the head of what Doctor Bowers calls neuropathic, that is, subject to some organic nervous disorder. The testimony in the case given by two or three witnesses from the depositions and from Alfred Hickman on the stand and Mr. Hickman on the stand showed that he was a man who was extremely eccentric, who could not control his temper, at one time given over to reading the Bible and at another time flying into rages and tearing everything into pieces. I don't know what that means. It means that there is neuropathic stock; there is an epileptic; and two persons, one insane in the last two generations of this boy's immediate family; and then this second cousin who was epileptic.

So it is conclusive, ladies and gentlemen of the jury, at the time of his birth, some nineteen or twenty years ago, at the time of his birth, when he came into this world, he was predisposed towards insanity and predisposed towards this particular insanity, dementia praecox.

Cantillon concluded his summation by addressing the issue of the possibility Hickman was faking his mental illness.

There has been some suggestion here that this boy has been coached into these delusions. I believe that Doctor Reynolds had the temerity to make that statement. I don't know. I don't think he has been coached. I know I have not done it myself. I am confident that none of my associates have done it. I know that Doctor Shelton would not do it. I know that we did not attempt to coach Mrs. Hickman on any questions of insanity. I will say that. I will say that we did not coach the grandmother. She was dead, I guess, before I was born. We did not coach any of these ancestors. And, speaking for myself, I know that I would not know how to coach anyone upon the subject of insanity.

After challenging the testimony presented by the experts from the prosecution Cantillon paused for a long time and then faced the jury. "Now, ladies and gentlemen, I think we have established that this was the act, not of a criminal, but of a madman. He is not a criminal, ladies and gentlemen; he is insane. I thank you."

CHAPTER 7

"You know what your problem is; it's that you haven't seen enough movies. All of life's riddles are answered in the movies."
Steve Martin—*Grand Canyon* (1991)

Mary Pickford was the original diva of the motion-picture industry. Several years before the kidnap and murder of Marion Parker there had been a failed attempt to kidnap Mary Pickford. The failed attempt was the subject of numerous newspaper editorials complaining about the moral decay of life in America. The Hickman case rekindled the sentiment, and the reporters who covered the trial frequently made comparisons between the two crimes. The idea being promoted by the media was this: if Mary Pickford was not safe, no one was safe. The tabloids covered this event from every angle, raising another issue, which actors still have to deal with today—to what extent do actors and famous people have private lives, and what issues should not be open to public scrutiny?

During the Hickman trial Pickford was involved in a dispute with the director D. W. Griffith. He offered her a part in one of his films and she responded by saying: "I'm sorry Mr. Griffith, but that part calls for bare legs and feet." It was not just the idea that Miss Pickford did not want to expose her bare legs to the camera that made her statement memorable. She was expressing in simple terms the crux of an argument that was dividing the motion-picture industry. The question was what was art and what was not. The question was highlighted by the fact that Congress believed they had a moral obligation to answer the question for the public, and the right to use censorship to support their point of view.

Louis B. Mayer fought the issue of censorship his entire career. For over three decades he engaged in one protracted disagreement after another with producers, directors, and stars over the issue of what was art for art's sake, and what was not acceptable for distribution by a major studio. Throughout the Hickman trial, Mayer maintained public silence. The issue of theater owners refusing to show newsreels that included clips about the Marion Parker murder case remained unresolved.

At the same time, Mr. Mayer was involved in one of the biggest disagreements in the early years of MGM. He was embroiled in an argument with a diva named Lillian Gish. To attract the actress to his studio, Mr. Mayer had agreed to pay her nearly a million dollars for a series of six films. He also allowed something few actors at the time could even have imagined was possible. He allowed her to select the parts she would play and to select both the director and co-stars.

After completing her first film without conflict, Mr. Mayer and the star disagreed on the second proposed film. Lillian Gish wanted to make an adaptation of Nathanial Hawthorne's *The Scarlett Letter*. It was reported that Mr. Mayer was dumfounded by the choice. He could not understand how a cultured lady like Miss Gish would even suggest a movie in which she would play a single woman in a family way. Mr. Mayer argued that the difference between a book and a movie is that the sophistication of the reader can be measured by their reading level, whereas a film's value and the viewer's degree of understanding depends on how vividly the studio presents the story.

Mr. Mayer also wanted the audience to feel sympathetic towards the actors and actresses on contract with his studio. Miss Gish saw the role of Hester in *The Scarlet Letter* not as a good or evil character, but as a female character in conflict. There were reports Mr. Mayer did not know the plot of Hawthorne's book. Both of his own daughters stated they had never seen their father read a book.

The reason Mr. Mayer was opposed to the film was because he believed it would increase the possibility of government censorship of the film industry. Lillian Gish successfully argued that the introduction of evil into a plot is sometimes essential to the story. In the finished film, Miss Gish played the part so successfully the audience had little difficulty distinguishing between who was truly good and who was evil. Critics loved the adaptation. The general audience hated the movie and the part Miss Gish played in it. Mr. Mayer hated the film even more when it failed to make a profit.

The lesson Mr. Mayer learned from the dispute altered his view on censorship. While quietly dropping the issue of theater owners failing to show the newsreels of the Hickman trial, he made the following statement in support of the Hays Code:

> The first class needs little care in handling, as sins and crimes of this class naturally are unattractive. The audience instinctively condemns them and is repelled. Hence the one objective must be to avoid the hardening of the audiences, especially of those who are young and impressionable, to the thoughts and the facts of crime. People can become accustomed even to murder, cruelty, brutality, and repellent crimes. In general, the practice of using a general theater and limiting the patronage during the showing of a certain film to adults only is not completely satisfactory and is only partially effective. However, mature minds may easily understand and accept without harm subject matter in plots which does younger people positive harm.

CHAPTER 8

"It is pretty easy to fool an audience with
a little crepe hair and a dialect."
W. C. Fields

According to reporters covering the Hickman case, the district attorney stood confidently before the jury on the morning of his summation, looking individually at each panel member without saying a word. As a savvy prosecutor he knew the jury was looking to him for clarity on the main issues of the trial. One by one, he knew he needed to draw the jury of twelve men and women to his way of thinking. He would use only the evidence already addressed in the trial to prove Hickman had been sane at the time he committed the crime.

Tension was abnormally high inside the courtroom. Mr. Keyes started his presentation with a subdued introduction. It was, by all reports, a strong performance using flawless and unencumbered logic. Mr. Keyes's delivery was slow and methodical through most of his argument. It wasn't until the ending of his argument, when he spoke of everyone's right to be skeptical of Hickman's insanity plea, that he unleashed a combative style of presenting the facts. Here his tone of voice became more and more incredulous as he accused Hickman of trying to distort the truth.

> I am not going to go into the horrible details of this crime, as counsel indicated to you that I might. I have no wish or desire to do that. When we started out to try this case, during the course of the trial I anticipated that it would be necessary for me, and I expected to have to prove to you and display before you some of the gruesome details. Counsel for the defendant has anticipated my move and beat me to the punch, as they say in the street, and prove those things himself.
>
> Why? He didn't fool me. I don't believe he fooled you. He wanted to prove to you that this crime was so horrible and gruesome that it might cause you to believe that no man in his sane mind could have committed it. Now those gruesome details are in the past. They are before you as evidence, and you can remember them just as well as I can. So I am not going to touch on them. I am not going to try to arouse your feelings against this defendant, because I state to you, ladies and gentlemen, thank God, that we live in America, and in America the laws of this great land say that every man or woman or child accused of crime is entitled to his day in court. He is entitled to be tried by his peers, by his fellowman. He is entitled to his defense. He is entitled to have reasonable time to prepare for his defense. He is entitled to go before a jury of his peers, and he is entitled to

show every single thing that may bear on his innocence, and the people are entitled to show every single thing before that same jury that may bear upon his guilt.

The district attorney stood up from behind the long table in front of the judge and moved towards the jury box. He was impeccably dressed and appeared to be considering his words carefully. His initial comments were related to his views on the nobility of American law. He supported Hickman's right to have a vigorous defense and complimented the ability of his attorneys. Raising his voice slightly Asa Keyes made it clear the issue was not guilt or innocence because the defendant admitted his guilt. The issue was simply whether or not William Edward Hickman was sane at the time he committed the crimes of kidnap and murder. The district attorney was mindful of the fact it was the first time the issue was raised in a California court under newly drafted legislation defining the legal implications of an insanity plea. He went on to assure the jury if he honestly believed Hickman or any defendant was insane he would encourage the jury to accept the insanity plea. Asa Keyes was adamant he believed the man who kidnapped and murdered Marion Parker was completely sane and deserved to be punished for his crime.

> But, from the very first, from the time I first set eyes on that man up in the jail in Pendleton, Oregon, I did not believe, and I do not believe now that that man was insane at the time he committed that kidnapping and murder, or that he is any more insane at this present moment than anyone else in this room. Therefore, in my own heart feeling about this defendant as I do, I have no hesitancy and no compunction in asking this

jury to bring in a verdict in this case that at the time this man committed this crime he was sane.

Now, then, that brings the issue right down to that one thing. You have been told that many times. I want you to bear it in mind, because you have no more to do with the finding of a verdict of guilty against this defendant for the commission of this crime, or not guilty of the commission of this crime, than you have with trying to stop Colonel Lindbergh from flying to the United States from where he is today. Your sole issue to determine here, ladies and gentlemen is this: was the defendant, on the 17th day of December 1927, at the time he killed little Marion Parker, as has been described in the evidence in this case, sane or insane. That is the issue. Plain and simple, isn't it?

Asa Keyes lowered his voice and complimented the jury for being attentive to a complex legal situation. Then he addressed the core issue of medical testimony.

Now, then, you know two gentlemen have been called here by the defendant to testify that in their opinion this man not only was insane then, but is insane now. They tell you that they made a through physical examination, and also subjected him to certain mental tests. I refer to Doctor Shelton and to Doctor Skoog. It would hardly seem proper on my part to stand here and try to take anything from the standing of these two gentlemen who have been called their standing in the community here or Doctor Skoog's standing in the community in Kansas City. I know nothing about either one of them. I never heard of Doctor Shelton before he took the stand in this case. I never heard of Doctor Skoog until he came out here and took the stand in this case. Knowing nothing about them, knowing nothing about their reputation or ability, I will not say one word against them. But I have the right, ladies and gentlemen, to direct your attention to one or two things as I have observed them from the witness stand.

You know Doctor Shelton, in his anxiety to prove to you that this defendant is insane and was insane at the time he committed this murder, took two-thirds of a whole afternoon in telling you the things that this defendant did not have. You remember that he took the time of this court and jury to go into every phase of dementia praecox that he knew of, and from the way he testified I judged he had pored over the same books that he said he was reading the night before, and committed a major part of them to memory. And he told you on cross-examination that the principle symptom of dementia praecox of the paranoid form was that this defendant had in his judgment that principal symptom or symptoms were mental delusions, were delusions and hallucinations. And Doctor Skoog said the same thing. Just bear in mind, I am going to come to that a little later. Now, Doctor Skoog came out here and first saw the defendant on the 26th of January. We started this trial on the 25th, I believe. That was the day after this case started that Doctor Skoog got here, and he gave the defendant examinations on the 26th and 27th, and he recited to you or read to you from his notes, and gave you in evidence here, some of the tests which he said he subjected this man to, this man Hickman.

Remember now that Hickman was arrested on the 22nd of December, and on the 24th of December, when the officers of the law from Los Angeles went to Pendleton to bring him back here, he started in with his insanity dodge. And I call it his insanity dodge advisedly, because I am convinced from this evidence that it is nothing more or less than a dodge on the part of this man in an effort to dodge the law. Remember this boy has intelligence. Remember that this boy is quite a smart young chap. He has intelligence, and his intelligence has not been impaired by mental disease of any kind, or any other kind of disease. He is just as smart now as he was when he took second place in that oratorical contest back there in the high school in Kansas City. He is just as smart now as he was when he graduated from high school in Kansas City with high honors. And he knew, ladies and gentlemen, when he was caught up there in Pendleton, Oregon, he knew that the only way he could escape the gallows or the penitentiary or the punishment which the law provides in the State of California was by the plea of insanity.

So I say to you that in my judgment, from that day to this, this defendant has made it his plan and his scheme to play this defense of insanity. And every single thing that he could do from the time when he was caught in Pendleton up to this time, everything that he could do to try to fool the doctors, to try to fool the judge, to try to fool the district attorney, and last and most important of all, to try to fool this jury, that man has been doing.

So then Doctor Skoog put him through his test. May I have Doctor Skoog's testimony for a minute? Of all the asinine tests that I ever heard of Doctor Skoog testified to them here on the stand. Remember now, this man had been talking to alienist after alienist. He knew the game. He knew what they were after. He knew when he was going to be subject to mental tests for somebody to come up here to testify he was sane or insane.

The district attorney received permission from the judge to read part of the doctor's testimony.

> The witness said the reason that he murdered Marion Parker instead of his mother was this: In everything he is the only one of the type. Now he says that he is greater than Jesus Christ; he has a greater message for the world than Jesus Christ. Jesus Christ had a message for the poor, but he has a message for everybody. And he said that if he had killed his mother, that that would just be a common, ordinary crime, that there had been lots of people that had killed their mother, but there had never yet been anyone who kidnapped a girl, taken her away, cut her to pieces, and threw her dismembered parts away; in other words, that that was done to bring the attention of the world to him. That is what Skoog says the defendant told him, that he killed this girl and cut her up and committed this crime the way he did for the purpose of bringing the attention of the world to him.
>
> Do you believe that, ladies and gentlemen? Have you any idea that the man who committed this crime had any such thought in mind at the time he took the parts of the body out to the father and grabbed $1500 out of his hand, with a gun pointed to him, and did what he did subsequent to that very moment? Did he stand up there and say, "I have been directed by a divine providence to commit this crime"? Did he say, "I committed this crime so the eyes of the world would be directed to me and be on me"? No, he did not do that.
>
> What did he do? Why, he did just as every criminal that I have ever known to do who had the opportunity to do it. He took the $1500 and put it in his pocket. He held up a man at the point of a gun, didn't he, on the

evening of the next day after which he had obtained this money, and he stole his automobile didn't he, and took what little money he had, and he did not even then, after he had committed that crime, with that thing on his mind and conscience, he did not even then ride down the street or go to the police station, or go anywhere else and say to the world, "I have committed this deed because I have been directed by divine providence to do it." And he did not go out and proclaim to the world that I have committed this crime; here I am; I am insane, and I want the eyes of the world to be upon me for the commission of this crime.

No, he did not do that; oh, no. He did just what any other criminal would have done under the same circumstance after having committed this crime. Why, he made his escape, of course; when he held up this Mr. Peck when he took his automobile, he was planning to escape and asked Peck's testimony, how much oil and gas the car had, how much oil, when did the oil have to be changed. He was figuring then on getting away, not of having the eyes of the world directed upon him, ladies and gentlemen, as he told Doctor Skoog was his motive for committing this crime; not that the eyes of the world might be directed upon him, but to seek cover, so that not a single eye, not a single eye of a human being on the face of the earth could see him or know him.

The district attorney took a moment to regain his composure while he placed the transcript of the testimony back on the prosecution table.

Doctor Skoog is the only human being who has testified in this case that this defendant ever, at any time, had any hallucinations. You know, those are hallucinations when you imagine that you hear voices telling you to do something. Those are hallucinations. Not a single word of testimony in this case, other than that of Doctor Skoog, who tells you that the defendant, on the 26th or 27th of January, told him that he had hallucinations. Not one word. Don't you think, ladies and gentlemen, if this defendant Hickman had really been having hallucinations, that voice had ever told him anything, or had ever talked to him, or even directed him to do anything in his whole life, down to the time he committed this awful murder, don't you believe there would have been some people here to whom he had communicated those thoughts, to tell you about them?

Asa Keyes was equally dismissive of the testimony of the only defense witness, Doctor Shelton. He turned his attention to the issue of the value of the prosecution witnesses.

As against those two doctors we have produced here men who have resided in this community, some of them for many years; men who have gained national reputations as alienists and psychiatrists; men whose honor and reputation cannot be questioned by anyone; Doctor Reynolds, Doctor Schorr, Doctor Parkin, Doctor Mikels, Doctor Bowers, Doctor Orbison, and Doctor Williams, many of them at this very moment members of the Psychiatric Board of the County of Los Angeles; many of them who are seated out there day after day, week after week, month after month, diagnosing the cases of people who come before the Lunacy Commission charged with being insane.

You have heard the qualifications from each one

of them as it was given to you from the witness stand. Do you believe that those gentlemen know anything about this thing that we are trying to find out about in this case, called insanity? Do you think they know anything about it? Why, here I have had Williams, Doctor Williams; pardon me for calling him Williams; he is a very estimable gentlemen. I have known him for years. He has testified on the stand, as he said, in cases both for me and against me, and when I say me I mean the People, represented by me as a prosecutor in a particular case. I have heard his testify in many a case, and I have tried to break his testimony down by cross-examination, and I knew what these young fellows were going up against when they tackled that fellow.

Why, he knows more in a minute about insanity than Walsh or I will ever know if we studied it from now until doomsday; and I am telling you, ladies and gentlemen, when I put that man and the rest of these gentlemen on the witness stand here I vouched for their integrity, and I am willing to stand by it until judgment day. Not only that; I vouched for their judgment. All of these men say that they have examined this defendant and they cannot find even the slightest evidence of dementia praecox, paranoid form, dementia praecox of any other form, or any kind of insanity in this man.

Now, the defendant, through his counsel, has built up here a beautiful picture of all the symptoms of dementia praecox, paranoid form. He has asked every doctor on cross-examination, and he asked his own medical men on direct examination, about all the symptoms of dementia praecox. That is all right. Let him ask them about the symptoms. There are many symptoms and the diagnosis of the disease, I believe, according to the testimony of the doctors, cannot be mistaken. I think Doctor Schorr testified to that, that you cannot mistake the diagnosis of a dementia praecox, paranoid form. Certainly there are symptoms. The trouble is with the defendant, ladies and gentlemen; he had built up a wonderful form here. You know, it reminds me of one of these forms I used to see in my wife's dressing room. I don't know who in the world made it for her, and it did not look any more like her than it does like me, but she used to hang dresses over it. These symptoms they bring in here remind me something of that. You can build a wonderful structure about paranoid dementia praecox, and she could build on that form a most beautiful gown if she were building it for herself, or making it for herself it would probably fit, but if she tried to make it for the little baby in the house it would not fit at all.

After summarizing the testimony of the prosecution witnessed, the district attorney did a review of the defendants personal history and concluded:

This man is not insane, ladies and gentlemen; he is not insane; he is bad; he is rotten to the core. Why do I say that? I say it for this reason: That we find that after he left this high school, after he left the parental roof, he commenced to commit very grave and serious crimes, and he was getting away with it. He was committing burglaries, grand theft, and robberies at the point of a gun. You know that is the history of every criminal, when he once starts it seems he never stops until Old Man Law in the shape of the sheriff, constable, or policeman grabs him by the collar, pulls him in, and puts him where he belongs. It is so easy, you know, after the first step is taken, it is so easy to go on, and it is such an easy way to make money, they think... they think!

That is what this man thought. He did not want to work; he did not want to apply himself to any such labor, but he chose the easier way, which leads to destruction. He tread that path, ladies and gentlemen, from that time until he was caught in Pendleton, Oregon, or near Pendleton, last December.

Now, during all of that time, during all of that time when he was committing these robberies and these burglaries and these larcenies, do we find any evidence in this case, has there been anything produced before you and, mind you, it would have been had it been available, to bring to you or to indicate to you that this man ever claimed to anybody that he was being guided by a divine providence in the commission of these crimes? No, you don't find one word. On the other hand, we have young Welby Hunt, who was his boon companion for about twelve months, and he was with him at the time Mr. Thoms, the druggist, was murdered over there on the east side, and murdered by this boy and Welby Hunt in the commission of a holdup. Why, he says they went in there to get money, that they wanted money, just another crime, easy to commit with a big gun on his person, with young Welby Hunt armed the same way. They go in there and rob Old Man Thoms's drug store, and in the commission of the robbery, a policeman who happened to be there commenced to shoot and the defendant and young Welby Hunt commenced to shoot, and Mr. Thoms was killed. Before they went in there, or after they got out, did this man Hickman utter one word to Welby Hunt that a divine providence was telling him to go into that drug store and rob it? Did he say one word to Welby Hunt that a divine providence told him to kill and slay a defenseless man in the protection of his prosperity? Did he say one word to Old Man Gurdane, the chief of police of Pendleton, Oregon, after he was caught, that a divine providence had told him to commit the murder on which we are now trying him?

You know that he did not, because Gurdane says that the Fox, when caught, like Old Man Adam of old, when he was caught in the Garden of Eden, blamed another. He did not even have the nerve and the temerity at the time to tell Gurdane that he had committed the murder. No, he said, "Oh, I kidnapped her, yes but a man named Cramer cut her up; I did not cut her up." Don't you see, ladies and gentlemen, don't you gather from what these doctors tell you about this dementia praecox, paranoid form, that a man who is really afflicted with that, that a man who really had it, that a man who really committed a crime guided and influenced and directed by his insane delusion tell you all?

At this point the district attorney described the circumstances following Hickman's arrest and made the point he did not initially make any reference to insanity.

Now, we have at first, as the evidence shows, he said, I want to plead guilty. I am going before the judge and plead guilty. I want a copy of this my confession myself to put before the judge, and I want also to make another statement to go before the judge, to tell him why I did it, to tell him why I did it.

Remember, now, he has been in the Pendleton jail up there for several days; he had been several days on the road up there; he was fleeing from the law; he was fleeing from the consequences of his act. Do you think that he realized and appreciated the nature and quality of that act that he committed? Do you think that he realized that the act, which he committed, was wrong? And, after all is said and done, ladies and gentlemen, when you get into the jury room, remember this, that whether you believe him to be a little off, or whether you think he is perfectly sane, as I think he is and was, that the test, under the law of the State of California and the law will be given to you by the judge, and I am going to cite it. In general the test is: Has he sufficient mental caliber, has he sufficient mental capacity to realize and appreciate the nature and character of the act he has committed? Yes he has.

All right then, has he sufficient mental capacity to know that that act was wrong and against the laws of the land? Why, it seems to me I am wasting my time, wasting my efforts here, when the thing is so clear and plain. Do you think that he would have run away under the circumstances that he did? Do you think that he would have assumed the name Peck the way he did when he got up to Pendleton, Oregon? Do you think that he would have stated that somebody else committed the crime? Do you think he would have tried to escape, if he had not realized the nature and character of the act that he had committed and if he had not known that it was wrong?

Why, when a lawyer, or a doctor, or any other man gets up before a jury and in the face of the testimony in this case as to the actions of this man, now, remember, ladies and gentlemen, the best way for you to find out and determine for yourselves whether or not a man, at a certain time was sane or insane, is by what he does and what he says. That is the only way these doctors can find it out. That is the way they do. They look at him; size up what he says and what he does. I want to tell you when eight of Los Angeles's best will give a man the examination these gentlemen they gave this man, and get up before a jury and, under their oath, testify that they can't find a single thing in the man indicating that he is insane, it means something to me, and when I find a man who has been doing the things that this defendant has been doing, who has been acting as he has been acting, and when he commits the greatest and most atrocious crime of all acted as he acted without displaying one single thing that tended to show or does show that his mind was other than a sound, reasoning mind, I want to tell you that I feel that I am wasting your time and the Court's time in any further discussion in trying to convince you that I am right, whether I am wasting time or not, I am going until twelve o'clock.

Let's see, this man with the great delusion, with the one delusion that he is guided by a supreme providence and that alone? Yes. When he wants to give his motives... he was not asked to do it, but he stated to the officers that he wanted to do it, it was going to be shown to the judge. When he is given that opportunity he sits down to write it out in his own word, in his own way and takes his own time. He said it, motives. After giving his name, and so forth, which you can read here if you want to, he says the first motive that comes into his mind, which, to my way of thinking, ladies and gentlemen, is the reason why he killed that girl, first, fear of detection by police. He did it in the belief that by killing and dissecting the body, he would be able to avoid suspicion and arrest. That is why he killed her. You know this man had been getting in his travels, in the commission of these various crimes that he committed; he had been getting some money. He killed this man Thoms out here in the drug store in December of 1926, do you remember, that is the testimony.

The very next month he goes to work down here at the First National Bank. He may have decided that after he killed that man it was a pretty serious thing, that he and Welby had better go straight. He may have decided that; I don't know, although I think he is a monster without a soul, without conscience, without a heart, but he may have decided to try to go straight, so they decided to go down to the First National Bank, where Mr. P. M. Parker was working, and they got a job as pages, both of them. They did that within less than two weeks after killing Mr. Thoms in the holdup. He did not go straight, however, for very long. Came a time he needed a motorcycle, or wanted a motorcycle, so he took to forging checks to buy the motorcycle and was discovered in his forgeries, brought up before the bar of justice and made no claim there, ladies and gentlemen, that a divine providence had guided him or told him to commit these forgeries, but he pleaded guilty and was placed on probation, taken back to Kansas City by his mother where he immediately commenced to engage in a life of crime; stayed there until November of 1927 when he came out here.

Now, listen, he was not getting enough money in his robberies, he was not doing well enough, so he concocted the scheme of kidnapping some young girl and holding her for ransom. Well, that is not the first time that that has been done. That crime has been committed since long before I can remember anything. My reading tells me that it is being committed every month in the United States today; someone is kidnapping, someone is kidnapping somebody. It is being committed down in Mexico, where they are kidnapping American citizens and holding them for ransom. That is the same thing this boy did. He says he wanted $1500 to go to college. I don't know, and I don't care whether he wanted to go to college with this money or not. He wanted the $1500, so he kidnapped Marion Parker.

Now, while he had her in his possession, while he had her under his control up here, he wrote several notes to the father. Great stress was laid by counsel the other day in examining Doctor Orbison about the character of the writing of these letters that he wrote at that time. Well, as a matter of fact, he did not write at all; he printed. He printed. Why? To disguise his handwriting so that his identity could be kept in the dark and his crimes could be hidden. Do you believe, ladies and gentlemen, that he was guided by divine providence at the time he penned these notes, these so-called "death notes" to the father of this girl, when he printed them instead of writing them?

Don't you believe, ladies and gentlemen, that if the contention of the defense were true and that this defendant were really actuated by and guided by, and controlled by, this thing which he has denominated providence, that he would have written those letters in his own handwriting and there would have been no attempt at concealment? Ah! The defense doctors, Doctor Skoog, I think it was, when asked if he thought this flight of the defendant, the printing of these letters and the other acts that the evidence shows that he did in trying to make his escape and getting away from the law, if those acts were comparable with the idea that this man was guided by this providence, he said yes. Well, Doctor Skoog, you remember, is the gentleman who was asked on the stand that if he had asked the defendant what the moon was made of, and if the defendant had said it was made of cheese, that he would have believed that was evidence of insanity.

So he got this young girl up in his room there, as the evidence shows and as he tells you ladies and gentlemen. Then he killed her because he was afraid that the officers of the law were on his tail, and he was afraid of detection. Now, that is exactly why he killed her, because he was afraid of detection. Why, you say, and the ordinary layman down the street say, I don't see how a man could commit a crime of that kind and be in his right mind. No, lots of people say that, you know they don't see how he could commit a crime of that kind and still be in his right mind. Well, these people have not had pictured to them, ladies and gentlemen, they are not apprised of, by word of mouth, the picture that you have had painted to you of the character of this defendant. He is a criminal; he is a bad man, he is a man without a soul, without a conscience, without a heart, and when Doctor Orbison or Doctor Williams, I have forgotten which, was asked the question as to whether or not he considered this defendant the ordinary American boy, his answer was no, thank God I do not. He is not the ordinary American boy, and I am telling you ladies and gentlemen, he is not the ordinary American boy, but he is a type of an American criminal which we have in this country, and which, with the aid of your verdict, the state of California will purge from her borders.

Now, when he was holding this girl, this man who does not believe in God, who believes that he is above the savior of mankind, according to his own story to Doctor Skoog this boy penned a note to the poor, suffering father and family of this little girl. In that note he told Mr. Parker that if he wanted aid to ask God, not man. Why did he do that, ladies and gentlemen? Why did he do that? He did that to instill in the father, in that father and that mother and that family the most awful terror and dread: If you want aid, ask God, not man. After he is caught, after his trail is ended, when he stands before the bar of justice, he tells you that he is asking aid from the divine providence, which he says guides him and controls him. Why, ladies and gentlemen, he wants to bewilder you, he wants to fool you, he wants to make you think that he was not responsible for the acts which he committed. Of course he does. He has not fooled me and I trust he has not fooled any of you.

I am going to leave this case with you, ladies and gentlemen, in a very few moments. This defendant has stated, in his contemplated speech which he prepared in the county jail to be given before the jury that he wants to be an example for American youth, but the whole trend of his thought in that speech which he had written out, and which he gave to Doctor Orbison, was that he wanted to escape the gallows. The best way for this young man to afford an adequate example to the American youth of today is to do with him ladies and gentlemen just what the law says should be done, unless there be some extenuating circumstances in the commission of his crime. The best example he can show to the people of the United States is that California, the far western state of this great United

States, say to people who commit crimes of this kind
that you cannot come within my borders if you have
sense enough and mind enough to read and realize
the nature and character of your act and to distinguish
between right and wrong, and commit a crime such as
this and be dealt with other than in the most severe
and extreme manner.

Fully aware that the outcome of the case would have a
significant impact on his chances of reelection, the district
attorney repeated the facts of the case, moving his arms and
filling the room with his voice. When the recapitulation was
finished he paused and lowered his head.

Positioning himself directly in front of the jury he said:

I am going to submit this matter to you at this time
with the hope, that it does not go out across the wire
to the Atlantic Seaboard, across there to Europe, the
other way to Asia and to the countries of the world that
Los Angeles County, and the State of California, are
not able to adequately cope with the criminals, because
criminal this man is and not insane.

From the reaction of the jury there was little doubt in
Asa Keyes's mind they would agree with his view of the
necessary verdict. The media was enamored by his effort
and praised his skills in print. Louis P. Mayer read the
accounts of the summation and was hopeful the issue of
William Edward Hickman and the refusal of theaters to
show newsreels of the trial was behind him.

CHAPTER 9

"You can't handle the truth!"
Jack Nicholson—*A Few Good Men* (1991)

With all the testimony given, all the forensic evidence addressed, and the summations completed, attention turned to Judge Trabucco, who was ready to deliver his instructions to the jury. Both the defense and the prosecution submitted to the bench the underlying legal issues they thought were critical to their side of the case. Judge Trabucco took their input into consideration and made his comments on each point in this historic case. He spoke for almost half an hour to the jury regarding the legal implications of the new California insanity legislation. As far as the question of Hickman's culpability, he told the jury what they had heard many times from both the defense and prosecution: The sole issue they must reach agreement upon was whether or not

Mr. Hickman was sane or insane at the time he committed the kidnap and murder of Marion Parker.

His instruction was precise and to the point.

> It is not every kind of degree of insanity which renders a person incapable of committing crime. Before you can find that the defendant was insane at the time charged in the indictment as of the dates of said offenses, you must find not only that he at those times suffered from insanity, but that the insanity was of that kind and degree which constitutes a defense to a criminal charge and which is more fully explained in the following instructions.
>
> All persons are presumed to be sane. If they are not, then they are in a diseased and deranged condition of the mental faculties as to render the person incapable of knowing the nature and quality of the act or of distinguishing between right and wrong in relation to the act with which he is charged.
>
> You are to determine what the condition of the defendant's mind was at the precise time of the commission of the act charged in the indictment.

Then the judge addressed a subject the lawyers knew was going to make or break their case. The issue of whose expert witnesses were the most believable. He instructed the jury by saying:

> The jury is the sole and exclusive judge of the effect and value of evidence addressed to them and of the credibility of the witnesses who have testified in the case. The term witness includes every person whose testimony under oath has been received as evidence, whether by examination here in court or through

deposition. The testimony of all witnesses is to be weighed by the same standard.

The character of the witnesses, as shown by the evidence, should be taken into consideration for the purpose of determining their credibility, that is, whether or not they have spoken the truth. The jury may scrutinize the manner of witnesses while on the stand, and may consider their relation to the case, if any, and also their degree of intelligence. A witness is presumed to speak the truth. This is a rebuttable presumption, and it may be repelled by the manner in which he testified; his interest in the case, if any, or his bias or prejudice, if any, for or against one or any of the parties; by the character of his testimony, or by evidence affecting his character for truth, honesty, or integrity, or by contradictory evidence. A witness may be impeached also by evidence that at other times he has made statements inconsistent with his present testimony as to any matter material to the cause on trial; and a witness may be impeached also by proof that he has been convicted of a felony.

A witness willfully false in one material part of his or her testimony is to be distrusted in others. The jury may reflect the whole of the testimony of a witness who has willfully sworn falsely as to a material point. If you are convinced that a witness has stated what was untrue as to a material point, not as a result of mistake or inadvertence, but willfully and with design to deceive then you may treat all of his or her testimony with distrust and suspicion, and reject all unless you shall be convinced that he or she has in other particulars sworn to the truth.

As the judge finished addressing the jury, a reporter wrote: "You could see every member of the jury became acutely aware that their time to pass judgment on Hickman's guilt or innocence was at hand." As if on cue, the news that the jury was beginning their deliberations went out to millions of interested Americans by way of radio. Despite the fact that District Attorney Keyes had performed like a superstar in his summation to the jury, the unpredictability of twelve citizens reaching a unanimous verdict brought many to fear the unthinkable. What if, after weeks of testimony from almost one hundred witnesses, after concrete crime scene evidence and numerous confessions, the jury found Hickman innocent based on his claim of insanity? The public did not have to wait long to have their concerns laid to rest. Forty-five minutes after leaving the courtroom the jury foreman reported back to the judge they reached a verdict.

Judge Trabucco ordered a dozen deputy sheriffs to be present in the courtroom for the reading of the verdict. Once they were in place he entered through the back hallway and took his seat behind the bench. He warned the audience he would not accept any show of emotion before or after the verdict was read. Anyone violating his order would be arrested on the spot. When there was complete silence in the courtroom he addressed the foreman.

"Has the jury arrived at a verdict?" the judge asked.

The foreman stood in response to the question. "We have, your Honor."

"Will you kindly hand the verdict to the bailiff? Mr. Bailiff, please pass the verdict to the bench. The defendant will stand as the clerk reads the verdict."

"In the Superior Court of the state of California in and for the county of Los Angeles, people of the state of California, plaintiff, versus William Edward Hickman, defendant, case number 325-43. We, the jury in the above, entitled action find the defendant herein sane at the time of the commission of the offense of murder charged in the indictment. Signed, James A. Ruggles, Foreman."

The clerk asked the jury, "is this your verdict, so say you one, so say you all? Please speak up audibly."

"It is," came the response from all the jury members. There was a hush inside the courtroom until a spectator got up, walked into the crowded hallway, and shouted, "They got the son of a bitch!"

Two weeks later Asa Keyes questioned Dr. A. F. Wagner and Chief of Detectives Herman Cline prior to the judge's sentencing. No new evidence was presented to the court during the penalty phase of the trail, just a restating of issues relating to Marion's mutilation and Hickman's behavior.

The judge listened intently then went directly into the reading of his verdict: "The court now determines and finds that the degree of crime in count two of the indictment is murder of the first degree without extenuating or mitigating circumstances. William Edward Hickman, stand up."

The attorneys rose from their chairs, appearing somber. The defendant stood, looking almost as if he were amused by the proceedings.

> It is the judgment and sentence of this court that for the crime of kidnapping, the offense described in count one of the indictment, that you William Edward Hickman, be confined in the state prison of the state of California, at San Quentin, for the term prescribed by law, which term will be fixed by the Board of Prison Director.
>
> Testimony was received by the court for the purpose

of ascertaining and determining the degree of the crime charged in count two of the indictment to wit, murder. The court, after due consideration determines and finds that the degree of the crime in count two of the indictment is murder of the first degree without extenuating or mitigating circumstances, and that for the crime of murder, the offense described in count two of the indictment, you shall suffer the penalty of death. Therefore, it is the judgment and sentence of this court, William Edward Hickman, that for the crime of which you have been convicted to wit, murder in the first degree, that you be delivered by the sheriff of Los Angeles County to San Quentin, to the warden of the state prison of the state of California at San Quentin, to be by him executed and put to death on Friday, the twenty-seventh day of April, nineteen hundred and twenty-eight, in the manner provided by the laws of the state of California. And may God have mercy on your soul.

Hickman's sentence of death left the judge no choice but to remand him to the only prison in California authorized to perform an execution. Hickman would spend his last days on earth in the 275-acre property known as San Quentin: a maximum-security prison located in the San Francisco Bay. Originally built in 1852, it was the oldest prison in California and at the time of Hickman's verdict all executions in the state were done by hanging.

Before Hickman's neck could be broken by the pressure of a hangman's rope, the sentence needed to be reviewed by a higher authority. The appeals process dealt with legal issues involved in the administration of the trial and not on the evidence given during trial. What the appeals court was looking for were prejudicial errors on the part of the judge, the prosecution, or the defense team.

When the State Supreme Court received the defense team's arguments for a mistrial they systematically reviewed twenty legal challenges before allowing the verdict to stand. There was nothing left for Hickman's attorneys to do but request that the governor of California step in and save Hickman from the death sentence. Neither Mr. Walsh nor Mr. Cantillon were optimistic about their chances. The horrible publicity the Hickman's case generated would have meant political suicide for the governor if he showed any mercy.

The defense attorneys made their request sent to the governor just weeks before Hickman's scheduled execution.

My Dear Governor Young:

On behalf of my client Mrs. Eva M. Hickman, of Kansas City, Missouri, mother of William Edward Hickman, who is under sentence to be executed in the State Penitentiary, at San Quentin, California, upon Friday October 19, 1928, I desire to respectfully petition you as follows: As Governor of the State of California, I ask you to command your great prerogative of clemency invested in you by the law of the State of California, and commute the death sentence heretofore imposed upon William Edward Hickman, to that of a sentence for the balance of his natural life, in the State's Prison at San Quentin.

If you will not accede to this request, I then beseech you upon the broad grounds of human justice to take the necessary steps to appoint a board or commission, of your own choosing from the ranks of the medical profession in the State of California or elsewhere of persons learned in the science and practice of psychiatry to immediately inquire and make investigation into the mental condition of William Edward Hickman and report to you before you as Governor of the State of California permit the forfeiture of the life of this unfortunate lad.

In this connection, regardless of the judgment of the courts of California, I positively assert to you that William Edward Hickman is an insane person. Too that he was for a long period prior to the time he so justly outraged the public conscience of California by his wholly incomprehensible deed, afflicted with that, the greatest of scourges know to the human family. He is unquestionably possessed of an insanity that is progressive in nature and one that all of the medical authorities agree proceeds in an insidious manner to a complete ravaging of the mental facilities, and finally to a total dementia. No unprejudiced person conversant with the facts surrounding this demented boy can say that he is type of person contemplated to be the victim of the capital punishment laws of the State of California.

Your Excellency will not gainsay the proposition that no sane person should be hanged. No intelligent person with a genuine appreciation of the real moral values of human life would advocate such a procedure. I therefore, consider that it will highly become your Excellency, as it will comport with the great dignity of your high office to adopt this request to make certain that a great stigma will not become fasten upon the fair name of California, that in the exaction of the supreme penalty from William Edward Hickman, will grow in the succeeding years to be an abhorrent and malodorous crime.

This boy is but twenty years of age—an age at which the great State of California, by its law, holds a person incapable of contract, or of disposing of their property, and many other kindred acts, and yet incongruously enough that very same law will impute to this boy sufficient mental capacity (conceding for the moment that he be perfectly rational) to admit of him performing acts that will work a forfeiture of his liberty, aye, even of his life.

Your Excellency is not without precedent in making a humane disposition of this case. In the great Commonwealth of Illinois, a case of monstrous circumstances involving boys of tender years was disposed of in a humane and righteous manner because of their youth, questionable mental capacity, and because of other circumstances. I make bold to assert that if William Edward Hickman is permitted to die, at your hand, in the face of the record and disposition of that case, it will in no uncertain measure be tantamount to both a state and national disgrace.

In conclusion, permit me to indulge the ardent hope that Your Excellency may be guided by an all-wise and provident God, in the discharge of this the most scared of your duties.

Respectfully submitted,

Jerome Walsh

Surprisingly Governor Young received hundreds of letters from concerned citizens asking him for clemency toward William Edward Hickman. He also received several thousand letters from people across the nation who demanded Hickman be hanged on schedule. The governor of California responded by saying he was not impressed or persuaded by any letter campaign and yet because of all the publicity surrounding the case he felt compelled to make a public statement. The statement put to rest any hope that Mr. Walsh, Mr. Cantillon, or Hickman's mother had for clemency.

> I will treat the Hickman case as any other that might come before me. I take the position in all matters such as this that the judge and jury and other officials who were in charge of the trial are in a better position to judge what action be taken than I, and as my duty to state dictates I will always sustain them unless some unforeseen circumstances arise to prove an innocent man is to be punished. Unless something new that would tend to establish the innocence of Hickman can be produced, I will not consider executive clemency. It is my fixed policy to presume that the courts and juries have ample means of determining the guilt or innocence of accused persons. The notoriety of the Hickman case does not differentiate it from any other case.

Hickman's supporters were critical of the governor for making his decision without resolving the issue of what part mental illness had played in the commission of this hideous crime. One supporter actually praised Hickman's behavior based on her new libertarian philosophy called Objectivism. Ayn Rand, the Russian born author of *The Fountainhead* and *Atlas Shrugged*, used Hickman's own words to describe her point of view: "What is good for me is right." She went on to describe his sociopathic behavior as "the best and strongest expression of a real man's psychology I have heard."

Ayn Rand's opinion on Hickman and his criminal activity was so extreme she lost some credibility among the growing number of people who embraced her philosophy of self-determination. She did not wavier in her support and continued to speak favorably about Edward Hickman and his behavior as if it were something noble in concept. In case someone got the impression she was only speaking philosophically about Hickman's hideous criminal behavior, she clarified her position in her published journal. "Hickman is born with a wonderful, free, light consciousness, the absolute lack of social instinct or herd feeling. He does not understand, because he has no organ for understanding, the necessity, meaning, or importance of other people."

Entering San Quentin prison, Mr. Hickman was treated like any other inmate. He was photographed, made to wash his body, and then received a standard haircut before being assigned his cell on death row. Along with the other convicted felons who arrived at San Quentin on that day, Mr. Hickman was given a number and became Inmate 45041.

He spent his last days talking with Dr. Leo Stanley, the chief surgeon of the prison. The doctor reported that Hickman's face was somber and his behavior was that of someone on a crusade. As the day of Mr. Hickman's execution neared Dr. Stanley continued to document their encounters with the intent of writing a book dealing with the general criminal population of San Quentin. Each time the two met, the doctor asked Mr. Hickman a series of open-ended questions, trying to determine if Mr. Hickman's behavioral indicators changed in any way. In response to one of his questions Mr. Hickman gave the following response: "The little girl's father made the mistake. He trusted me.

That was silly of him. He should have telephoned the police the minute he knew she was kidnapped, in spite of my note warning him not to, because no crook plays fair, and I am a master crook."

The doctor also made notes of several occasions when Hickman spoke with contempt for both Mr. Parker and his daughter Marion. Dr. Stanley reached the professional conclusion that Mr. Hickman believed everything he was saying to be true. The doctor also concluded Mr. Hickman was delusional, and possessed an unlimited capacity for self-deception. Dr. Stanley even wondered if Mr. Hickman had heard any of the evidence in his own trial. The prisoner still did not realize Mr. Parker had brought in the police at the very beginning. Based on their conversation it was clear to the doctor that Mr. Hickman believed he had controlled the kidnapping process from beginning to end. He believed he was the one who had pulled the strings that made everyone involved act the way they did.

Without any factual evidence to back up Mr. Hickman's bizarre behavior, the prison doctor began to see Mr. Hickman's responses as purely narcissistic, a behavior which allowed Mr. Hickman to find refuge from the reality of his life. The doctor also felt Mr. Hickman was no longer internalizing his pent-up anger and was perhaps for the first time revealing the man behind his convoluted effort to appear insane.

When asked by Dr. Stanley why he had murdered the young lady, Mr. Hickman changed his response from his pre-trial testimony.

"It was this duel force," Mr. Hickman was adamant, "I

think, the impulse to harm anyone I cared for, and the desire to execute a master crime, that made me kill her."

Dr. Stanley reported that he asked his next question question looking for some kind of remorse on Hickman's part. "Are you sorry for what you did?"

The answer came without ambiguity. "No, I felt no pity for the father. I felt no remorse at all. I just felt I was executing a masterstroke. As for the little girl, she is better off than I am. At least she is out of this world of turmoil and strife. I no longer believe in a heaven or hell, but I know we shall have everlasting life." During this short outburst, Dr. Stanley said Mr. Hickman showed himself lacking any regard for the welfare of others. Everything about the kidnapping and murder was about him and him alone.

CHAPTER 10

"Mama always said life was like a box of chocolates.
You never know what you're gonna get."
Tom Hanks—*Forrest Gump* (1994)

As the year of 1927 came to an end, the authorities in the province of Montreal, Canada, were still unable to name a suspect in the fire that took the lives of seventy-seven children at the Laurier Palace Theater. The grieving parents continued to speculate, hoping the government would keep the case open until they discovered the truth behind the tragedy. Their optimism was starting to fade. Without any new witnesses or evidences, the case quickly fell from national attention. As the public outrage died down, the Royal Canadian Mounted Police closed the investigation, and it was never reopened.

The ongoing concern of the Catholic Church about the influence of movies on children led to the creation of the Legion of Decency in 1934. Those who supported the Legion took a pledge in church to boycott morally objectionable movies. As part of the pledge they agreed to avoid theaters with a reputation for showing films banned by the Legion. Initially the Legion had a strong influence on film production, and producers kept their criteria in mind as they made films directed towards large audiences.

Within a decade after its creation the influence of the Legion diminished. In 1957 Pope Pius XII issued an encyclical called *Miranda Prorsus*, calling for the Legion of Decency to stop banning films and to concentrate on promoting films that promoted Christian values. In response to the Pope's directive the list of banned films eventually morphed into a rating system. By the 1960s the Legion of Decency found its influence on Hollywood to be negligible.

In 1975 the Legion of Decency was shut down and replaced by what is called the Bishops' Catholic rating system. Currently the Bishops' list appears to be random and has little influence on the current production of films.

Following the Hickman trial the film industry created its own rules called the Motion Picture Production Code, formalized in 1930. The code provided specific guidelines for subjects like religion, sexuality, and violence. The rules were commonly referred to as the Hays Code, named after the former Postmaster General Will H. Hays, who became the president of the Picture Producers and Distributors of America. He was responsible for creating and enforcing moral codes used to guide the production of films. As the man in charge of the distribution of films for studios, he was in a position to determine which films would be available and which films would be unavailable to theater owners.

Hays hired Joseph Ignatius Breen to work as a troubleshooter for the Code Commission. He was initially hired as a go-between for the Commission and the Catholic film censors. Breen eventually took on the role of code enforcer. Louis B. Mayer was not supportive of Breen's appointment, because the man had no hesitation in expressing his anti-Semitic views. After World War II Breen expressed concern that Jewish filmmakers would offend German Americans by making anti-Hitler films. His method of enforcement was his ability to impose a $25,000 fine on studios that released films without the Commission's seal of approval.

Breen's role was affected in the fifties by the emergence of a foreign film market with independent distribution. The code was also threatened by the competition from television. The final challenge to the code came from the Supreme Court decision to ban filmmakers from owning theaters. With such a crack in the strong hold major studios once held on the industry, independent producers like Howard Hughes and Otto Preminger completely ignored the guidelines created by the code. These guidelines were created by the industry and were not legally binding. Since studios no longer had leverage as theater owners to enforce the code, the rules were no longer considered part of the filmmaking process. The influence of moral considerations was replaced by target group marketing surveys designed to cater to public taste.

During the sixties the pretense of using moral guidelines for the creation of films was dropped. This opened the floodgates for the creation of films based on subject matter that was previously considered inappropriate. At the same time, parents were starting to notice the influence of television advertising on their children. In 1952 ads for Mr. Potato Head generated $4,000,000 in profit for Hasbro in its first year of production. It was an unprecedented number for children's toys, and created the first red flag for parents concerned about the influence of media on childhood development. In response, the Children's Television workshop was created in 1968, to address the use of media for educational purposes.

More recently this concern has shifted from the influence of television to the influence of computer-generated media. The debate on this influence continues. The core issue is whether or not over-indulgence in electronically based forms of stimulation diminishes a child's ability to effectively engage in critical self-evaluation, or if it creates a tendency to live in a delusional world created by fantasy. The exact same question raised at the trial of William Edward Hickman.

• • •

Within days of Mr. Hickman's conversation with Dr. Stanley, in which he denounced Mr. Parker and Marion's part in the kidnapping, his fragmented psyche allowed him to find God with the help of Father William Fleming, the chaplain at San Quentin. As a converted Catholic, Mr. Hickman began a writing campaign, trying to contact everyone he had ever wronged. He wrote to those he robbed or took advantage of, asking his victims for their forgiveness. One of these letters went to Mrs. Thoms, the wife of the drugstore owner Hickman had killed in his first robbery attempt in California. It read:

Dear friend,

I do not wish to hurt your feelings at this time and I am most sorry for having caused you any past grief. You know that I am facing death. I am a wretched sinner but I believe in the salvation of Jesus Christ, our Lord. I want to try to reconcile any differences between myself and others so far as I am able. Please do not be bitter against me. You trust in God and he will bless you if you do not hate anyone. Of course, you have a very good cause to be indignant against crime. However, I hope you will not hinder your harmony with God by bitterness.

I am writing this letter from a purely Christian standpoint. I do not hold anything against anybody. I wish you joy and happiness and wish Mr. Oliver [the LAPD police officer] the same. God loves us all. I have opened my heart to him. I repent and praise Jesus for my deliverance. I hope everybody will love and serve God so that all violence and injury will cease. I do not ask any favors for my own self. I ask you to pray for us condemned men here at San Quentin for the glory and in the name of our Lord. Please ask Mr. Oliver to do the same.

I believe Mr. Thoms is living in the spirit of Christ and you can meet him in Heaven. Life is eternal through the Son of God.

A contrite and humble sinner
W. E. Hickman

As the day of Mr. Hickman's execution got closer, he was allowed to address the media one last time. He returned to a theme he had expressed earlier when he told reporters: "I want no young man to study my crimes. My life has been deplorable. I think the publicity given to crooks and crimes has a bad influence. It should be given to men and women of high purpose who deserve it."

Then he handed out his last written statement.

> Crime and other evils are signs of ignorance and death. All criminals and unrighteous men are struggling in the clutch of satanic error. By willful disobedience to God's law they become ignorant of the laws of truth and life. All creation is based upon positive force. Such is the will of God. However, the devil is exerting his influence upon the minds of men in order to tear down the work of God. By the defeat of Satan crime and violence have come into the world. Men who will fully reject Jesus Christ and deny the grace of God have ultimate damnation and torment...

> The reason that I became such a horrible criminal was because I allowed a demon of hell to lead me on. I praise God for lifting me up out of the pit of darkness and corruption. I was most ignorant...

> I beg young people to keep a close watch over their morals. Cling to the Christian faith and practice. Then you will have a solid foundation upon which to build a good life...

> Jesus Christ is the only way, truth and life. Let all evildoers think on this. Do not let the devil deceive you any longer. May God bless the people of the United States.

On October 19, 1928, at ten o'clock, the warden of San Quentin allowed the doors to the room holding the prison's gallows to be opened for a viewing by the media. The high ceiling accommodated a large platform with thirteen steps from the floor of the gallows platform. The California Penal Code Section 1229 clearly states "the warden, a physician, the attorney general, twelve reputable citizens selected by the warden, five relatives or friends and one minister were to observe any execution." The room was built to accommodate less than a hundred people. Over two hundred people were present to view the hanging. The notoriety surrounding the Hickman case had persuaded the warden to suspend the rules so all interested individuals could see for themselves the end of a notorious criminal's life. The audience was a mixed group of public servants, press, and the curious who pulled whatever strings they could to see the hanging of the decade. Carroll Peeke was there as a reporter and wrote a description of Hickman's death:

> When Hickman appeared at the east door of the gallows room, his lips were mumbling the responses to a prayer, which Reverend Frank A. Fleming was reciting. The moment he entered the room, the doomed man flung his head back, apparently to look up at the scaffold. His head remained held back until the black cap was slipped over it. With his arms strapped stiffly at his sides, the young man was rushed up the thirteen stairs to the gallows by two guards, each holding a hand under the armpit.
>
> The two guards, Charles Alston and Fred Hageboom, held the youth on the trap door while Robert Hageboom, the hangman, brother of the guard, adjusted the noose, the black cap and the straps about his legs. Father Fleming stood nearby reciting the Litany, but Hickman seemed to have lost all capacity for hearing or for any formal response. Head still strained

backwards, the young man's lips framed voiceless words against his hood, and those in the crowd of some 345 persons who stood nearest believed that the words were, "Oh, my God! Oh, my God!"

Then standing there on the trap he collapsed as the guards withdrew their hands. His knees slipped, and his whole body tilted down to one side. The guards at the bottom of the gallows steadied him with their hands.

But at this second, and it was only 22 seconds since Hickman had first appeared at the door and caught that one sight of the gallows, the hangman raised his hand. Three men hidden behind a low partition on the back of the gallows, sitting there in a little room awaiting the signal of the uplifted hand, slashed three cords with their knives.

One of those cords released the trap and with a clang it fell. The condemned youth, because he had been about to fall to one side when the trap sprung, struck one foot against the side of the suddenly opened aperture as he fell, and the blow knocked off the slipper from that foot. The body dropped violently downward to a perpendicular position, but before it could start swinging a trusty rushed forward, placed his hand against the back, and held it steady.

Dr. Ralph Blecher stepped forward into a small roped-off area at the foot of the gallows, mounted a little stepladder and ripped the white shirt of the suspended man open at the neck. Then he applied the stethoscope and listened carefully. Dr. L. L. Robinson held the pulse. Hickman's hands during the first few minutes clutched convulsively.

Detective Lucas of the Los Angeles Police Department, who obtained Hickman's confession after the murder of Marion Parker, already had fainted before that convulsive movement of the young man's fingers commenced. While the doctor listened through the stethoscope, the crowd wondered what went on behind the black cap, whether the fall had broken Hickman's neck or whether he was strangling to death.

• • •

After the conviction and execution of William Edward Hickman, Asa Keyes was the talk of not only Los Angeles but of most of California. He was made speeches on the need for law and order, addressed service clubs, and was the guest of honor at political dinners organized to raise money for his upcoming campaign. Keyes wanted to keep the momentum from the Hickman trial going by achieving one more success in the courtroom before the elections.

A month after the successful prosecution in the trial of the murder and kidnap of Marion Parker, District Attorney Asa Keyes returned to the case he had been working on before the kidnapping. C. C. Julian was a well-known oilman who traveled around Southern California promoting his oil company to the point of selling more stock certificates than the company was worth. C. C. Julian was a Canadian who had traveled to the United States to work in the Texas oil fields.

In 1921 Julian had relocated in Southern California. Promoting his skills as an oil rigger he managed to convince a handful of investors to buy a vacant lot in Los Angeles. He set up five oil wells in the lot and they all produced oil. His investors made significant profits and Julian became a celebrity in the city's newly expanding oil-production community. From that point on, Julian concentrated his efforts on finding new investors and selling stock in his company. His sales campaign included daily advertisements in local newspapers. Julian's flamboyant style came to the attention of investors from Hollywood, including Louis B. Mayer, who encouraged the actors on contract to his studio to make similar investments. The media treated Julian like a movie star, closely following his personal life, including the coverage of a nightclub fistfight with comedian Charlie Chaplin.

The sale of stocks in the C. C. Julian Oil Company was known as a Ponzi scheme. Julian would pay off the initial investors with money collected from new investors. He managed to keep the scam going for four years until it collapsed. Investors were skeptical of company explanations of the collapse and demanded a criminal investigation. Remarkably, a lawyer from Texas named S. C. Lewis and his partner Jack Bennett took over the oil company, fired C. C. Julian, and kept the scam going for another two years. When the company collapsed a second time it came under investigation by the Los Angeles district attorney. Asa Keyes led the investigation until the murder of Marion Parker made headlines. At that point he dropped the fraud case and concentrated on the kidnapping trial.

When Keyes was ready to reopen the C. C. Julian case he claimed most of the witnesses had disappeared and went to court to have the charges dropped. At that point forty thousand residents of Los Angeles had been swindled out of an estimated $150 million. It was a con of unprecedented proportions and the subject of national news.

In January of 1928, Asa Keyes entered a Los Angeles courtroom and asked Judge Duran to drop all charges against S. C. Lewis and Jack Bennett. The judge was incredulous and accused the district attorney in court of incompetence.

Reaction in the media was split. The *Examiner* was ambivalent. The *Times* attacked Asa Keyes with a vengeance. There were rumors Otis Chandler, the owner of the paper, had lost money in the scam. The bad publicity from the *Times* caused Asa Keyes to lose his bid for reelection.

The first order of business for newly elected district attorney Buron Fitts was to open an investigation on Asa Keyes based on allegations of corruption in office. The *Times* reported Keyes had accepted a bribe of $30,000 from the evangelist Aimee McPherson to drop charges of perjury against her during the investigation of her alleged kidnapping. When Fitts failed to take action in the McPherson case, the *Times* printed excerpts from the diary of Milton Pike, the owner of a clothing store located across the street from the Los Angeles courthouse. The clothing store was a well-known location for paying bribes related to court cases.

The testimony from Pike made it clear Asa Keyes had not only accepted bribes for dropping charges in the Julian investment case, but he also made specific requests for expensive gifts and the payment of a mortgage. District Attorney Fitts gave Jack Bennett one of the former owners of the Julian Oil Company immunity in exchange for his testimony against Keyes.

On February 9, 1929, in their morning edition, the *Times* reported one-time District Attorney Keyes was found guilty of accepting a bribe by a jury of his peers and sentenced to fourteen years in San Quentin. The *Times* made the following statement in their editorial in March of 1930:

> For probably twenty of the twenty-five years during which Mr. Keyes was a public official, he deserved and deserves, far more praise than blame. As a deputy district attorney, under the direction of a superior, he was a good lawyer, an efficient, honest and able prosecutor, winning the friendship of those with whom he came in contact and the respect of the public. His elevation to command in the office where he had long been one of the chief supporting pillars was, it may now be seen, a tragic mistake. He acquired bad habits, neglected his work, fell in with evil companions, put his trust in subordinates who betrayed him, and at last his liquor-weakened moral fiber yielded under stress of temptation and he was lured to final destruction.

Keyes was also investigated but not charged with failure to prosecute the main suspect in the killing of William Desmond Taylor, the movie director whose death helped trigger the Hays Commission. *Time Magazine* reported the downfall of Mr. Keyes in their March 24, 1930 issue. It said in part: "In the first years he was the district attorney of Los Angeles Asa Keyes sent 4030 men and women to California prisons for a variety of crimes. Last week he joined this criminal company himself, entering San Quentin Prison as a convicted bribe taker, a betrayer of public trust."

The magazine reported the following statement made by Asa Keyes as he entered the prison gates: "What is life? We have an hour of consciousness and then we are gone." Just like every other common criminal, Mr. Keyes was ordered to bathe, have his hair clipped short, be photographed and fingerprinted, given a number, and then assigned a jail cell. He was known from that day forward as 48218. The only courtesy shown the former district attorney was his assignment to a single cell in the "Old Men's Ward" by Warden James Holohan, as a safety consideration against possible retribution by prisoners sent to San Quentin by the once-district attorney.

Asa Keyes served just three years of his sentence in prison, with another two years of parole following his early release. The *Los Angeles Times* newspaper, which had praised him constantly during the Hickman trial, criticized the judicial system for letting him out after serving so little of his sentence. Their article read in part: "For the crime of accepting a bribe by a public official in so responsible a position, and upon whom so much of the public welfare depended, nineteen months of imprisonment, even though it followed thirteen months in the County Jail, is obviously inadequate."

The newspaper article was the least of Asa Keyes's problems. Unable to practice law as a convicted felon he tried his hand making a living selling cars, then working as a bail bondsman, and finally by whatever means possible. It was reported by family members that his last paying job was with the movie industry, where he used his skills as a lawyer to advise writers and directors on how to script courtroom scenes in films. While working as a consultant for the film industry he was given a small role in one of the movies made by Louis B. Mayer at MGM.

Asa Keyes died of a stroke on October 18, 1934. Harry Carr, a reporter for the *Los Angeles Times,* wrote about his death: "I used to go to school with Asa Keyes. His was the greatest tragedy with which I ever came in personal contact. Asa was not a brilliant scholar; he had a careful, slow mind which worked things out. In later years he turned out to be one of the finest trial lawyers ever to adorn our district attorney's office. There is something poisonous about politics; it poisoned him."

The next day the *Oakland Tribune* wrote:

> You see, when Keyes was Los Angeles district attorney he was very sympathetic to Hollywood's problems. After he was released from the penitentiary, Hollywood sought to give him a helping hand. He began as an automobile salesman and the stars, headed by Lew Cody, bought his cars.
>
> Then came the cycle of trial pictures and the men behind the gun had an idea. Why not let a real lawyer, like Keyes, play the losing lawyer in the court scenes. His voice was a good microphone. He knew the legal phraseology. So Keyes made more than pin money, but his back was always to the camera. Only once did I see him turn. That was recently for a fleeting moment.

• • •

LAPD Chief James Davis, one of the members of Hickman's original escort party from Oregon to Los Angeles, suffered a setback. His first tenure as chief of police lasted only three years because of his involvement in the scandal surrounding the Wineville Chicken Coop Murders, a criminal case adapted for the movies by Clint Eastwood in the film *Changeling*. Angelina Jolie played a mother whose son was kidnapped by a young man and, as in the Parker kidnapping case, the Los

Angeles Police Department failed miserably in their attempt to find the criminal. When the LAPD began to fall under pressure to solve the case they knowingly substituted another boy for the kidnap victim. While Davis escaped prosecution for his involvement in the hoax, several of his police officers were expelled from the force for taking bribes. Four years later, in 1933, Davis was given a second chance as chief of the LAPD and served for five additional years. His second tenure ended when two members of the LAPD Vice Squad were accused of placing a bomb under the car of a former LAPD detective who had agreed to testify in front of a grand jury for an investigation into corruption in the Los Angeles Police Department.

• • •

Jerome Walsh went back to Kansas and continued to practice law. Little else is known about him. Richard Cantillon became one of the most respected lawyers in Southern California. He met Asa Keyes in court once again in his very next case, where Cantillon successfully defended one of the investors in the C. C. Julian Oil Scandal. After his retirement, he sat down and wrote about the Hickman trial. The result of his efforts produced a well-written account of what it was like to take on an unpopular client in a day before the general public understood human psychology. The book was titled, *In Defense of the Fox.* It was published just weeks before his death.

Ray Nazarro, Cantillon's law clerk, left the law practice after the Hickman trial and went to work for Columbia Pictures as a screenwriter, director, and producer.

• • •

Louis B. Mayer did not go gently into retirement from the empire he helped build. In 1944 he faced his last challenge to the industry he loved. The threat came from the acceptance of television by the general public. Like he had not anticipated the invention of sound in movies, Mr. Mayer did not anticipate the public spending their time and money being entertained at home. His failure meant the MGM board of directors forced him to retire.

With few options left, Mr. Mayer tried his hand as an independent producer. He had a few successes but not enough to make a go of it. When he drove off the MGM lot for the last time he left behind an organization encompassing over 170 acres with thirty fully equipped sound stages. This was more than twice the number of any of his competitors. There were dozens of warehouses filled with millions of items, all saved and preserved so that they could be used in the making of future films and television programs. His replacement would inherit a group of men and women committed to maintaining props for both interior and exterior shots to meet the increasing demands of weekly television shows.

History has recorded the true asset of MGM as the long list of notable actors and actresses Mr. Mayer discovered, nurtured, and promoted. George Cukor commented on the accomplishment: "Louis B. Mayer knew the coin he dealt was talent. He would husband it and be very patient with it and put up with an awful lot of nonsense if he really believed in it. Of course, he was tough, and he could be ruthless and very disagreeable but he and Thalberg built up this extraordinary concentration of talent, which was MGM, and when Mayer left, the whole studio began going to pot. I think people don't see how a place like MGM had to be fed, sustained, and organized every day."

While in semi-retirement, Louis B. Mayer witnessed the end of his era when the Supreme Court in 1948 ruled on the case of the United States v. Paramount Pictures, Inc. This ruling forced all studios to sever any and all connections between themselves and their movie theater chains, reversing the business model Marcus Loew had created forty years earlier.

Mr. Mayer died on October 29, 1957, from the effects of leukemia. The one-time control freak, the man who had spent all of his adult life trying to dominate the film industry, left everyone wondering what he really meant by his last two words, "Nothing matters." But sadly Mr. Mayer died like the mythological character in Citizen Kane, who upon uttering his last word, "Rosebud," collapsed into unconsciousness, never to speak again.

• • •

In 1927, justice was swift. Less than a year passed between the day Mr. Hickman killed Marion Parker and the day he stood on the gallows. The official autopsy on Mr. Hickman reported he did not die of a broken neck, but suffered for several minutes until he died from traumatic asphyxia brought on by neck compression. Medically, this was the exact symptom found to be the ultimate cause of death for Marion Parker. It was reported that many who watched Hickman's body twisting and turning for almost three minutes came to believe justice was singing, "An eye for an eye."

The issue of whether or not Edward Hickman was affected by his prolonged exposure to the fantasy world of Hollywood was never fully resolved by the state-appointed doctor at San Quentin because Hickman was hanged so soon after his arrival. Eight decades have passed, and the bigger question facing the movie industry, television, and the makers of video games today is how the behavior of the general population is being affected by the ever-increasing violence seen in their respected media. Is the gratuitous violence depicted on the silver screen and on television having an adverse affect on the general population, or do violent images by their nature attract violent individuals and only reinforce their anti-social behavior? In today's entertainment we often see excessive acts of violence driven by the storyline; even movies with superheroes sometimes solve plot-driven problems with individual acts of violence.

As in 1927, the federal government is getting involved in this issue as lawmakers question the industry regarding the effect films might be having on the nation's children. Social learning can be defined as learning either values or behavior from role models encountered in one's everyday environment. When an individual spends large amounts of their free time interacting with movies, television, and video games, their primary social environment becomes their media of choice and not their family or community. In the case of Mr. Hickman, his personal life took a turn towards isolationism, and his values developed according to what he saw on his daily visits to the theater. In his own words, he justified his violence against storeowners with the fact that it brought him the financial rewards critical to his survival and lifestyle. In his dealings with Marion Parker, Hickman saw violence as a means of resolving the conflict he was experiencing with Marion's father. He felt no hatred towards Marion. This transference of hate and extreme violence by an individual towards innocent bystanders is repeating itself today.

On July 20, 2012, James Eagan Holmes was arrested and charged with killing twelve people, and wounding seventy others at a movie theater in Aurora, Colorado during a midnight screening of *Batman: The Dark Knight Rises*. Holmes confessed to the shooting. His reference to identifying with a film character called the Joker prompted the writing of this book.

• • •

When Mr. Hickman's body was placed into the ground the only people present other than the gravediggers were Richard Cantillon and Jerome Walsh, Hickman's two attorneys. No family members were in attendance.

Mr. and Mrs. Parker had their daughter's remains cremated after the autopsy. A simple service was conducted at Forest Lawn Cemetery for family and close friends. All the headlines, all the public interest, all the efforts made to capture and punish William Edward Hickman were eclipsed four years later in March of 1932 by the crime of the century: the kidnapping of Charles A. Lindbergh's child. Soon after the body of Lindbergh's child was found, the Congress of the United States passed a law making kidnapping a federal crime. From that day forward the Federal Bureau of Investigation became the lead agency in all matters pertaining to kidnapping of American citizens.

BIBLIOGRAPHY

Affron, Charles. *Lillian Gish: Her Legend, Her Life.* New York: Scribner's, 2001.

Altman, Diana. *Hollywood East: Louis B. Mayer and the Origin of the Studio System.* New York: Birch Lane, 1992.

Balcon, Michael. *A Lifetime of Films.* London: Hutchinson, 1969.

Barry, John M. *Rising Tide: The Great Mississippi Flood of 1927 and How it Changed America.* New York: Simon & Schuster, 1997.

Berg, Scott A. *Goldwyn,* New York: Knopf, 1989.

Cantillon, Richard. *In Defense of the Fox: The Trial of William Edward Hickman.* Atlanta Georgia: Droke House/ Hallux, 1972.

Chaplin, Saul. *The Golden Age of Movie Musicals and Me.* Norman: University of Oklahoma Press, 1944.

Crafton, David. *The Talkies: American Cinema's Transition to Sound 1926-1931.* Northbrook: Prime, 1999.

Carey, Cary. *All the Stars in Heaven: Louis B. Mayer's MGM.* New York: Dutton, 1971.

Crowther, Bosley. *Hollywood Rajah: The Life and Time of Louis B. Mayer.* New York: Holt, 1960.

Doherty, Thomas. *Pre-Code Hollywood.* New York: Columbia University Press, 1999.

Eames, John Douglas. *The MGM Story.* New York: Crown, 1982.

Eyman, Scott. *Lion of Hollywood: The Life and Legend of Louis B. Mayer.* New York: Simon & Schuster, 2005.

Eyman, Scott. *Mary Pickford.* New York: Donald I. Fine, 1990.

Flamini, Roland. *Thalberg: The Last Tycoon and the World of MGM.* New York: Crown, 1994.

Higham, Charles. *The Merchant of Dreams: L. B. Mayer, MGM and the Secret Hollywood.* Boston: Dutton, 1993.

Holden, Anthony. *Behind the Oscar: The Secret History of the Academy Awards.* New York: Plume, 1994.

Kinn, Gail and Piazza, Jim. *The Academy Awards: The Complete History of Oscar.* New York: Black Dog and Leventhal, 2002.

Letter from Jerome Walsh to Governor Young dated October 16. Preserved by the California State Archives.

Levy, Emanuel. *All about Oscar.* New York: Continuum, 2003.

Montreal Gazette: Issue, January 10, 1927.

Musser, Charles. *The Emergence of Cinema: The American Screen to 1907.* Berkeley: University of California, 1994.

Neal, Gabler. *An Empire of Their Own: How the Jews Invented Hollywood.* Anchor, 1989.

Newton, Michael. *Stolen Away.* New York: Pocket Star Books, 2000.

Parkinson, David. *History of Film.* London: Thames and Hudson, 2012.

Parrish, Michael. *For the People: Inside the Los Angeles District Attorney's Office 1850-2000.* Los Angeles: Angel City Print, 2001.

The Los Angeles Times: Issues December 19, 20, 21, 22, 23, 24, 25, 28, 1927, October 11, 17, 1928, March 1, 1930, October 18, 1934. In addition to these dates the newspaper's headlines for 1926, 1927, and 1928 and their stories were used as references.

The New York Times: Issues, December 19, 20, 21, 24, 29, 30, 31, 1927, January 2, 10, 26, 1928. In addition to these dates the newspaper's headlines for 1926, 1927, and 1928 were used as references.

Transcript of the Hickman trial vol. 1, vol. 2, and vol. 3, preserved in California State Archives.

Schlesinger, Arthur M. Jr. *The Almanac of American History.* New York: Barnes and Noble. 1993.

Time Magazine. March 24, 1930.

Wiley, Mason and Bona, Damien. *Inside Oscar.* New York: Random House, 1996.

ACKNOWLEDGMENTS

I would like to thank the following individuals
for their help with this manuscript:

Gene Barbic	Juan Ruiz
Kent Colwell	Jerry Tripp
Steve McCambly	William Stubblefield
Earl Nash	Sarah Masterson Hally
Rita Zulpo Rancano	

I want to thank Randall Klein at Diversion Books for supporting this project. I want to thank Sarah Jacobson for her tireless copyediting and the ability to see what I missed. I want to thank Chris Mahon for promoting the book, and I want to especially thank my agent, Rita Rosenkranz, both for her guidance through the process and for her impressive attention to detail. May the good work of talented people in the world of publishing continue to provide us with the blessings of the written word.

CPSIA information can be obtained
at www.ICGtesting.com
Printed in the USA
BVOW03s1245111116
467567BV00002B/4/P

9 781682 303276